BLOOD
AND
GLORY

THE CROSS IS STILL THE CRUX

STEVE HAWKINS

Dear David
Much blessing
to you.
Steve

CREATION
HOUSE

BLOOD AND GLORY by Steve Hawkins
Published by Creation House
A Charisma Media Company
600 Rinehart Road
Lake Mary, Florida 32746
www.charismamedia.com

Design Director: Bill Johnson
Cover design by: Terry Clifton

Library of Congress Control Number: 2013957297
International Standard Book Number: 978-1-62136-725-3
E-book International Standard Book Number:
978-1-62136- 726-0

While the author has made every effort to provide accurate telephone numbers and Internet addresses at the time of publication, neither the publisher nor the author assumes any responsibility for errors or for changes that occur after publication.

First edition

14 15 16 17 18 — 987654321
Printed in the United States of America

CONTENTS

FOREWORD

OFTEN AS CHRISTIANS we get busy doing the work of the Kingdom and are in danger of forgetting the importance of the cross in our lives. Where the streets are flowing with sacrificial blood, we are led to ponder the spiritual power that there is in blood sacrifice, and Steve's book is a timely reminder that the cross needs to be central in everything. No matter how mature we are in the faith, we can never sidestep or get beyond the cross; the reality of salvation, abundant life, and a growing relationship with Jesus is found only in the cross. Giving us an inside look into the blood-stained Temple courts of the Old Testament filled with the bleating of sheep and goats, past Muslim and Hindu festivals incredible power that there is in the blood of Jesus. Steve reminds us over and again that Jesus willingly shed His blood because He loves us and longs for an intimate relationship with us; He shed His blood so that we could be partakers of His glory. We are invited to take a fresh look at our lives and see if we are truly living in the reality that is now ours because of Jesus' shed blood on the cross. As you contemplate afresh Jesus' sacrifice and shed blood for you on the cross, I pray that you will have a fresh revelation of what this means for you personally. May you walk more fully into the reality that He has made available for you and find your true identity in Him. May Steve's book inspire us all to settle for less no longer, that Jesus' sacrifice may not have been in vain.

—PAULA O'KEEFE, FOUNDER,
LIVING WATERS HEALING COMMUNITY,
ARMAVIR, RUSSIA.

Introduction

THE CROSS IS STILL THE CRUX

D O WE SPEND too much time considering the Cross of Jesus? Is there a place to say we need to "move on"? If God is doing a "new thing" in our days, where does that leave the Cross?

We live in the twenty-first century. Historical and philosophical analysts describe the days we are living in as "postmodern." The following paragraph is a little wordy, but please read it. The Electronic Labyrinth comments:

> Let me give you the example of Californian culture where the person—though ethnically European, African, Asian, or Hispanic—searches for authentic or "rooted" religious experience by dabbling in a variety of religious traditions. The foundation of authenticity has been overturned as the relativism of collage has set in. We see a pattern in the arts and everyday spiritual life away from universal standards into an atmosphere of multi-dimensionality and complexity, and most importantly—the dissolving of distinctions.[1]

There are efforts far and wide, in these uncertain times, to draw people together, regardless of creed or color, indeed, to "dissolve distinctions."

Much of this effort is to be lauded. That people will give time and commitment to working on behalf of others, seeking to emphasize what different groups in society have in common and producing resources with which communities may work toward diffusing barriers and quarrels, is commendable.

In Christendom too there is a longing for unity, *real* unity. Jesus promised that we would know it as a reality. We see His expectation of this powerfully in the Gospel of John:

> Holy Father, keep them in Your name, the name which You have given Me, *that they may be one even as We are.*
>
> —John 17:11, emphasis added

> I do not ask on behalf of these alone, but for those also who believe in Me through their word; *that they may all be one*; even as You, Father, are in Me and I in You, that they also may be in Us, so that the world may believe that You sent Me. The glory which You have given Me I have given to them, *that they may be one, just as We are one*; I in them and You in Me, that they may be *perfected in unity*, so that the world may know that You sent Me, and loved them, even as You have loved Me.
>
> —John 17:20–23, emphasis added

It is one of the many outcomes and benefits of the finished work of the Cross. Jesus prayed that we would be "one" prior to going to the Cross, just as He and the Father are one. This is what was on His mind prior to the ordeal of His extreme suffering.

He saw glory beyond the shedding of His blood.

Many issues face the church today: discussions concerning women priests, the place of homosexuality in the church, and the issue of further integration of Catholic and Protestant arms of the church. At least, this is what the public generally sees from the media as being major issues. Society is changing by definition. Today, in fact, this very day, royal assent has been granted to the legalization of same-sex marriage in the United Kingdom.

Moreover, in the church of Jesus Christ, men, women, and children are hungry for the *reality of relationship with Jesus*, one that supersedes church attendance, activities, and traditional rites. As our hunger for Him is revealed, we find that reading the Bible and even moving in the gifts of the Holy Spirit in themselves do not satisfy. As important as these facets are, at our core we *want to know a Person. Him. God. One on one. Him in all His fullness.*

Much of the time we may be unaware of it, but in truth, we are gasping for Him. As a deer pants for water, so our soul longs for Him (Ps. 42:1).

Nevertheless, there is one inescapable truth that will always stand. It will always stand on earth because it forever stands in heaven.

It is this.

There is no reality of the real Life of Christ (I will use a capital L throughout this book since I wish to recognize that this Life is the life of Christ, His life in us as Christians) *outside of the Cross of Jesus Christ.*

Jesus Himself described the gospel as one that offends. It is indeed a narrow way into the kingdom of God. We also need to consider that His supernatural Life that follows adoption into His family is only available to those who align themselves with the Cross.

We do not leave the Cross behind after our first

confession of Jesus or on the anniversary of our initial year's church membership. We do not mature in our faith so as to leave the Cross at some kind of elementary "level." We never get beyond the Cross because Christ's Life is unequivocally yoked to it.

To grow in Jesus, we need the Cross in all things. If we are seeking an increasing, widening, and growing move of God, it is going to come as we appropriate all that has been accomplished at the Cross.

Paul admonished the Galatians for so readily allowing themselves to become bound, having first found freedom in the Cross. As usual, Paul doesn't mince his words. He called the cause of such complacency "witchcraft" (Gal. 3:1).

We are also going to see that the Christian Life not only begins with the Cross, but never loses sight of it. It is in the Cross that we truly find His Life and the power to live it, to live that *exchanged* life, to live the new life in place of the old one that has been crucified.

The Cross is still the crux of the matter.

Crux

n. pl. crux·es or cru·ces

1. The basic, central, or critical point or feature: the crux of the matter; the crux of an argument.

2. A puzzling or apparently insoluble problem.[2]

We are going to examine both of the aspects defined above: the fact that the Cross is central to everything in our relationship with Jesus Christ and our Christian walk; and that, for some, efforts to sidetrack the Cross can and will only lead to interminable frustration and, as the definition states, insoluble problems. Sidelining the Cross does lead to insoluble problems, for sure.

I pray that you will be blessed as you read and that you will receive impartation from the Holy Spirit, who is given to us that *revelation* may come our way and that we may receive truth. He is the truth, and He sets us free in every respect.

The Cross is not just for beginners in the faith. The Cross of Christ is the crux of the abundant life promised us by Jesus.

1

WHAT HAPPENED AT THE CROSS?

I T DOES NOT take much discernment to recognize, as you read the Gospels, that Jesus endured considerable opposition not only in His ministry of teaching, healing, and raising the dead, but also in His progress toward the ultimate goal of His earthly tour as "God made man." The agonies preceding and during His torture and death, it goes without saying, constituted appalling punishment as He finished the earthly part of His, literally, awesome ministry.

Awesome has become such a regular term for describing anything from a sports result to the quality of an ice cream. But Jesus really was awesome; He left observers open-mouthed by the words He said and the things His hands did. He was speaking and acting from a different place than that of those around Him. He had a different dynamic to Him when compared with the dynamic of the religious leaders of the day.

So often the unseen activity and battles in the spiritual, heavenly realms are far more significant than what is, or what appears to be, being played out here on earth.

Jesus always knew that He was going to the cross. I have heard it argued that this may not have been the case, that perhaps the God-man Jesus learned this from His Father during His time on earth. I would dispute this. Let's remember that Jesus visited earth in the Old Testament as well as in the New. In addition, as those who have ever received Him as Lord and Savior are described as having been chosen before the foundation of the world, it seems to me inconceivable that the Son did not know how their redemption was going to be achieved.

For men to be redeemed, to be saved from eternal and temporal destruction, an eternal price had to be paid. Old Testament accounts remind us that huge quantities of blood (of oxen, sheep, rams, and goats, among others) were shed to cover the sin of God's people. The Epistle to the Hebrews looks back to the Law and is clear when it states that there is no forgiveness without the shedding of blood (Heb. 9:22).

Blood and Violence

Glossing over many of the details in some Old Testament accounts (and there are books with a lot of very specific details!) can rob us of valuable insight into kingdom business.

I am not a particular fan of Quentin Tarantino's filmography. But if you have a taste for, shall we say, over-the-top blood and gore, I understand that Tarantino's your man. I have just seen my first Tarantino movie; I was not particularly aware that *Django Unchained* was one of his productions, but having seen a trailer, I had been looking forward to watching the film as soon as it was issued on DVD. I have to say it was a cracking, good watch! I do not wish to reveal any plot spoilers—but I will say this; if you have ever wondered what a room spattered with blood could look like, this movie provides you with an example!

Can you imagine almost countless numbers of animals being slaughtered as offerings according to the Law of Moses? Hundreds of thousands of them, even, on some festival occasions! The priest would even pick up limbs of the animals and wave them before the Lord as a "wave offering" in addition to the regular practice of sprinkling the altar with blood. These pieces of meat were not as we often find them at our local supermarket, wrapped in cellophane and placed in neatly labeled little polystyrene, rectangular trays! The blood must have been dripping and splish-splashing everywhere!

Blood. It is powerful.

> For the life of the flesh is in the blood, and I have given it to you on the altar to make atonement for your souls; for it is the blood by reason of the life that makes atonement.
>
> —LEVITICUS 17:11

The New Testament then assures us that a new covenant between God and men was inaugurated through the shedding of Jesus Christ's blood. This "once and for all" sacrifice, mirrored dimly in the catalog of Old Testament animal slaughter, paid the final, ultimate price to reconcile God and men; to literally dissolve their sins, atone for their sin nature, provide a new nature, and provide holistic healing.

> But now in Christ Jesus you who formerly were far off have been brought near by the blood of Christ.
>
> —EPHESIANS 2:13

All these benefits are to be accessed through an act of faith on the part of the sinner—the sinner being the one as yet distanced from reconciliation and relationship with God. The sinner admits his or her need, receives the gift of a new nature, and in so doing is transferred out of the kingdom of darkness and into the kingdom of light, God's kingdom, where Jesus Christ is Lord (Col. 1:13). Once the sinner has taken this step of faith, God exercises His part; He reconciles the individual by adopting him or her to Himself. He becomes part of the kingdom of God and the family of God. He changes nature; no longer does he retain an identity as a "sinner," but he has not become a "saint," a called-out one, one set apart to God.

Sinners do not become saints by what they do. They become saints by what God has done. The Bible says that having received Jesus, we receive power to live as children of God (John 1:12).

THE DIVINE EXCHANGE

You may have heard this phrase "the divine exchange" before. I like it. We hand our tainted stuff—indeed, all of our stuff over to God—and He hands us His stuff. We get a quite astonishing, never-to-be rivaled deal. Talk about "hitting the jackpot."

Despite knowing our nature, our behavioral record, and our ignorance of many of the realities concerning the transaction, God nevertheless offers the deal. All those who will accept it benefit from its terms.

We are literally transplanted spiritually. We are transferred from one kingdom to another. We breathe the fresh air of a new realm, one that was previously off limits. We were barred from it; now we have free access. We have become a new creature. All the dross that pertained to the former one is swallowed up in a new identity.

The gospel is very good news!

However, too many Christians live their lives as a struggle; some seem to struggle as much as or even more than they used to before they came to Christ! The Christian life for them is a slog, a toil, and largely hard work. Many strive to become who the Bible already confirms that they are. Many strive to impress a God who has already accepted and confirmed them. We will return to this theme later.

For now, let's take a look at the Cross from a wider perspective, especially at the lengths taken across religion and belief to disregard and avoid it.

2

HIGH PRICE

RECENTLY THE VIVIDNESS of what may have occurred during the Passion of Jesus Christ has been brought into a new awareness through its portrayal in Mel Gibson's film *The Passion of the Christ*.

Arguments have been had concerning the gruesome depiction of Jesus's treatment at the hands of the Romans especially. It is worthwhile to focus, for a moment, on the physical experience endured by Jesus, who, let us remember, is not only the Son of God but also the Son of Man.

He underwent monstrous, barbarous treatment. You could not wish it upon your worst enemy. That He persevered and saw it through is, in my book, nothing less than heroic.

I want to tell you something. Jesus Christ is my hero. He fully deserves such a title, too often today tossed at a personality who has fleetingly caught the eye of the media for some lesser reason.

He endured the punishment because He was motivated by love. This love had and has such an extraordinary, immeasurable depth to it that it would not let go of its goal. It would not give up its desire; such was its *passion*.

Passion speaks. I received a lovely comment this year

from one of my students at the end of her course. (I teach English as a second language in a further education college in London.) In her card to me she wrote: *Your teaching is a work of heart.*

Conversely, I remember a comment made in one of my early school reports! It suggested that while I was good at showing a healthy level of enthusiasm for my studies, such energy was not always backed up by "solid work." I seemed to be proficient at starting work but less so at seeing it through to the end.

Well, Jesus did a solid work, all right. No act could have shown, or has ever shown, more commitment than that once-for-all act of sacrifice.

The measure of His love is evidenced by the measure of quite atrocious brutality that He endured. The prophet Isaiah saw the Son of God in a vision hundreds of years prior to the event. He saw Him in the depths of His suffering. As you read these words in Isaiah, they are not quoted to, in any way, provoke a sense of guilt or shame in you, but rather one of gratitude and *release* as you see with the eyes of your heart *how much you are worth.*

> Surely our griefs He Himself bore,
> And our sorrows He carried;
> Yet we ourselves esteemed Him stricken,
> Smitten of God, and afflicted.
> But He was pierced through for our transgressions,
> He was crushed for our iniquities;
> The chastening for our well-being fell upon Him,
> And by His scourging we are healed.
> All of us like sheep have gone astray,
> Each of us has turned to his own way;
> But the LORD has caused the iniquity of us all
> To fall on Him.

He was oppressed and He was afflicted,
Yet He did not open His mouth;
Like a lamb that is led to slaughter,
And like a sheep that is silent before its shearers,
So He did not open His mouth.

—Isaiah 53:4–7

Verses 4–5 read this way in the New Century Version:

But he took our suffering on him
  and felt our pain for us.
We saw his suffering
  and thought God was punishing him.
But he was wounded for the wrong we did;
  he was crushed for the evil we did.
The punishment, which made us well, was given to
  him,
  and we are healed because of his wounds.

Love kept His mouth shut. This would have quite astonished His accusers. The Romans were used to such "trials"; times were turbulent. The norm would have been for an arrested man to vehemently protest his innocence in a desperate attempt to court favor and avoid such harsh punishments.

His love kept His mouth closed. He could have called upon legions of angels to strike down His enemies, but He knew that in so doing, He would have sidestepped the cross and therefore prevented us, undeserving as we are, from being reconciled to the Father in the kingdom of heaven.

In Gibson's film, a roller coaster of emotion amidst numbing portrayals of systematic abuse, the scourging of Jesus has drawn wide attention and comment. It may help us to consider this for a moment. I am not interested in glorifying gore for its own sake but to highlight to your heart that you, personally, *were worth it*. I want to bless you with revelation of that in His name.

SCOURGING

Scourging was not just a whipping. I imagine that a beating at the hands of trained Roman soldiers would have been dreadful enough. Like me, you may have seen other depictions of this element of Jesus's suffering; in such scenes He is beaten, and as the punishment ends, several red welts are evident across His back.

However, the Bible tells us that the punishment meted out to Jesus was such that He was unrecognizable as a man. Isaiah wrote:

> Many people were shocked when they saw him.
>   His appearance was so damaged he did not look
>   like a man;
>   his form was so changed they could barely tell
>   he was human.
> —ISAIAH 52:14, NCV

In *The Passion of the Christ* we get a depiction of a scourging, not a beating. Scourging was administered by two very focused agents of torture. Each of the soldiers had a *flagellum,* a whip of leather thongs interlaced with pieces of material such as glass, stone, or lead. Make no mistake about it; some victims never made it to their cross. Strokes from this instrument cut deep into the flesh, even to exposing bone.

I could describe further but—enough. I don't want to so fill the page with details of a nature that could repulse

readers, and as I have said, the message here to be empha-
sized is about a love for you and those around you, a love
that refused to lie down so that it *would* lie down, roped
to a wooden beam.

Jewish law stipulated that a prisoner could receive up
to thirty-nine strokes, the maximum actually being set at
forty. Thirty-nine were counted so as to ensure (ironically)
that the due punishment was not exceeded. It is unlikely
that Jesus would have been graced with such consider-
ation because He was not scourged by the Jews, but by the
Romans. In Mel Gibson's depiction, after many strokes
with a cane-like stick, Jesus hauls Himself back to His feet
to the astonishment of the Romans overseeing the sen-
tence, who then turn to the *flagellum*. It is as if He stands
to receive more punishment—that amount required to
satisfy Isaiah's prophecy that we would be healed by His
stripes (Isa. 53:5).

Do you know how much you are loved? Do you really
know? Holy Spirit would love to show you. He wants to
reveal that the Cross is a conduit of intimacy and not one
of religion.

3

RELIGION

TWO PARTICULAR STREAMS of thought beckon me when I consider the place of religions across the globe. First, religions evidence the fact that men are looking for God. We could put it another way; they reveal that *God is looking for men to return home to Him.* Second, there is an enemy, a personality, a fallen angel who is seeking to stop men from finding relationship with God. He is also seeking to prevent God from connecting with men. As this enemy, known as Satan (or the devil), has no power over God in any respect, his only option is to attack the other party in the equation, namely, people.

In my first book, titled *From Legal to Regal,* I devoted some pages to describing the ramifications of the two trees in the Garden of Eden. Having eaten of the tree of the knowledge of good and evil, men were henceforth doomed to live from a place of judgment and reasoning rather than as previously, when they had led a simple, satisfied life in partnership and in relationship with God through revelation in their oneness with Him. They did not need any knowledge outside of the revelation they freely received in relationship with their God.

The Fall, as it is known, was about much more than the

consumption of a piece of forbidden fruit. It changed men forever. It changed their thinking, and it changed their very identity and sense of it; no longer (until Jesus arrived on the scene) could they walk hand in hand with God. Life was now going to be hard work, one of toil, and a comparatively empty experience. The fall of man, from a secure position and from an identity in the Father to an orphan-like state away from Him, was a devastating one not only for mankind but also for the Father, who longed to "father" and nurture His creation from a place of intimacy.

However, eternity is set in the hearts of men (Eccles. 3:11), and although the struggles and busyness of life keep many isolated and deaf to the deeper cries of their hearts, this inner need to "be by God" does surface. It is almost impossible to keep it down. The inner voice may be distant at times, but it speaks nevertheless.

WORTH

I sometimes flinch when I watch talent programs such as *The X Factor*. Apart from the actual performances, we viewers are sometimes provided with a profile of the prospective star-to-be. It's wonderful to see family and friends offering such devoted support but also depressing to witness the candidates placing (at times) such desperate hope on the outcome: "I want this so much; I want them to be proud of me..." And the tears begin to flow...

Are we really so dependent on others for our sense of worth?

There is a place where we can know who we are. It is not dependent on our apparent achievements or upon the opinions, plaudits, or criticisms of others.

This book is not the place to describe the manner in

which a wide range of religions have come into being; your own research (if you are so inclined) will enable you to find out their roots. But I think it is fair to assert that religions start from the base point of an unmet need, a *hungry heart*—someone was seeking God. On occasions, in the search for the "other worldly," people have also sought to fill the inner void by partaking of "experimental" (let's call them) substances. This can open the door to the demonic realm. Let us remember, also, that there is an active adversary (who appears as "light") seeking to steer people away from the only true mediator, Jesus—indeed, to steer them to anyone or anything but Jesus.

Life is only in Jesus:

> I am the way, and the truth, and the life; no one comes to the Father but through me.
>
> —JOHN 14:6

Satan does not want to lose anyone to Jesus; this is a true statement, as Satan has been given temporary authority on earth. He has not yet been bound so as to be inactive. Unless one has received the authority to overcome him through belonging to Christ, one remains under his dominion.

If Satan can keep you away from Jesus altogether, he will try to do so. But if not, after you have come to Christ, he will seek to meddle with you, to counter the work of the Holy Spirit in your life. The Holy Spirit is working to transform you as a kingdom citizen. Satan will seek to undermine your appreciation of the destiny that is yours in Christ and of the riches that would flow to you from heaven. He might try to convince you that there is something laudable in living as a pauper, when in fact you are a prince.

In short, he will try to separate you from the Cross in any way that he can.

So Many Beliefs

It's a smorgasbord out there. There are the well-known religions such as Islam, Hinduism, and Buddhism, and also a whole raft of lesser-known and lesser-understood belief systems. It's a religion buffet. But one thing is not on the table of religion. Or if it is, it is on the corner of it, where hungry fingers are unable to reach it.

The Cross of Jesus Christ

Today, as I write, I saw an advertisement on Facebook for a Buddhist hub. The advert said that they offered "an easier, softer way." Such promises may appear attractive to the spiritual seeker, but there is no Life outside of the Cross. Satan promised Jesus the very same thing. In the wilderness he suggested that Jesus take another route to establishing a kingdom. And as late in His time on earth as in the Garden of Gethsemane, Jesus battled with the reality of what He was about to face. The enemy did his utmost to deter Jesus from going to Calvary.

I remember once seeing a depiction of Jesus at Gethsemane in a movie. Satan comes to Him and offers Him a way out. "Jesus, You don't need to do this; You don't need to put Yourself through such agony. It's so unneces-sary..." was the tone of the temptation. How reasonable the enemy must have sounded!

Satan wanted to destroy Jesus, but he did not want

Him to go the cross, where He would fulfill Scripture and defeat him *once and for all!*

The enemy is happy for people to immerse themselves up to their neck in religion, especially if they believe that there is salvation in it for them. Religions, let us not deny it, are behind a tremendous amount of valuable community and welfare work. They support community cohesion in some respects. Much of the teaching inherent in their belief systems can benefit those who listen.

But there is no salvation outside of the Cross of Jesus, nor is there the genuine Christ Life.

THE LIE

The lie is that religions have any God to worship *at all.*

The Bible says that all idols, or in other words, all things or people or "gods," are *nonexistent things.* That's right; the focus of their worship *does not even exist.* The Bible does not teach that people of different religions are worshipping the same God by different names. It says that there is one God and one God only, being as a Trinity, and that all other gods are nonexistent.

Our battle is not against flesh and blood, we read in Ephesians. This is primarily a spiritual issue, a spiritual dynamic that we are engaged with here. Satan masquerades as an angel of light, as a persona of wisdom, mystery, and promise. The reality is that he is a demon who, knowing that in due time he will be consigned to eternal imprisonment, endeavors to mislead people through his jealousy of Jesus.

And through his jealousy of us—men, women, and children—he knows that he can never inherit what is on offer to us: sonship, redemption, intimacy with Father, Son and Holy Spirit, and everlasting peace in our spirits.

So, to the empty-hearted, a religion may seem to be a worthwhile investment. It would be a mistake to believe that religions have no power; Satan is not powerless. To those who are insecure and fearful of what is happening in their lives and around them both nationally and internationally, being part of a large group of people with a religious identity promises comfort and a degree of control.

The reality is, however, that these spiritual movements are mirages. Closer inspection of them through the light (who is Jesus) of the Bible and the Holy Spirit reveal that there is nothing really there of substance.

4

LET'S GET TOGETHER!

THE BIBLE DESCRIBES all men as sheep. Have you ever watched sheep? I love them; seeing them out on a hillside, especially the young lambs, is a welcome sign that spring is "springing" and that warmer weather is on the way! Now, you may appreciate that is not always the case in the UK, but we press on in hope!

Sheep are naturally timid, aren't they? One moves, and the others pack in close and move with it. They are fearful, insecure animals who come to rely heavily on the voice of the one, the only one, they dare to trust: their shepherd.

Sheep follow sheep too. The Bible describes humanity as a flock of sheep that has gone astray; worse still, as sheep who have gone their own way. A sheep cannot become much more lost than that! Without the shepherd and the rest of the flock, it can but bleat and wait, hoping to be rescued.

There is a strong public voice in these days encouraging people of different faiths and persuasions to "come together." In the name of mutual respect and tolerance, people are being encouraged to look for the similarities in each other's creeds and to mingle, to show that the "spirit of man" is able to overcome all barriers and join as one.

"Seeker" groups with names such as Spiritual Awakenings, Enlightened Within, and Self-Transcendence litter social contact networks such as Facebook.

There are conflicting agendas here. As believers we simply have to view such persuasions through the Holy Spirit spectacles that we have been given to wear. Millions of individuals would love to see a peaceful, tolerant world. But there is a spiritual enemy who is working to bring a conformity of belief for *his* own benefit. Satan is described as the prince of the power of the air; the world's airwaves are, daily, filled with fear mongering that attempts to reinforce humanity's insecurity. While the advancing gospel rarely gets a mention, the loudest voices are those calling for compromise of belief for the sake of each and every one of us.

This does not pose, in effect, a huge problem for followers of *religion*. Although we see regular examples of the damage done through religious infighting, either between people of different religions or between those of various sects within a religion, the call for tolerance for different creeds grows stronger.

Satan is content for people to remain in the darkness of religions. One day the world will see apparent moves toward tolerance and even a form of unity on an unprecedented scale; this masquerade will try to convince the public that "all roads lead to the top of the mountain. One creed is no better than the other." This will actually be a deception sent to distract people from Jesus, the only way, truth, and life.

I have been working among people of different faiths for the last fourteen years in my role as tutor in the further education college I referred to earlier. It seems to me that Muslims, for example, are generally quite happy for

Hindus to be Hindus and for Christians to be Christians; I do not hear Buddhists questioning the Muslims' faith; those raised as Catholics appear to take no issue with any other faith walk, although for some of them, non-Catholic Christian streams are viewed with an element of suspicion and wariness.

As I write, Islam seems to be generating the most publicity around the world for brutal crimes perpetuated in its name. And yet an Islamic website comments:

> The dealings of the Prophet…with other religions can best be described in the verse of the Quran: "To you be your religion, to me be mine."
>
> The Arabian Peninsula during the time of the Prophet was a region in which various faiths were present. There were Christians, Jews, Zoroastrians, polytheists, and others not affiliated with any religion. When one looks into the life of the Prophet, one may draw on many examples to portray the high level of tolerance shown to people of other faiths.[1]

Religion, in its nature, tolerates religion. Religions are unnecessary where men are reconciled to their Creator!

But the Holy Spirit spectacles we wear show us a different picture concerning attitudes to Christians.

Inside and outside the parameters of so-called religion born-again believers are under fire. They are different in that they proclaim that there is only one way to salvation. This sets them apart. Satan is looking to ally all faiths and creeds together against the true church of Jesus Christ. The ironically named New Age movement is in essence not new at all; it is a mishmash of ancient occult beliefs and practices, designed and propagated by Satan to keep people spiritually active but in the realm of darkness.

There are many genuine, spiritual seekers among the followers who are looking for reality, meaning and freedom.

Jesus is not absent from the creeds of some of these faiths. He is there, but He is not there *as He is*. So, in an apparent, immediate contradiction, we should say that Jesus Christ is not there. There is no finished work of the Cross.

The current emphasis on and celebration of tolerance is, in truth, an attempt to disregard the Cross of Christ. It is an attempt to take a shortcut, to manufacture a (fake) unity between people and peoples.

I said in a previous chapter that there is no genuine unity outside of the Cross of Jesus Christ. That's right. Man-made efforts may impress and have the appearance of efficacy, but history shows us, and the Bible confirms, that such initiatives exist only on the surface.

We may all wear the same color jacket, but that does not mean our hearts are one. Only the blood of Jesus can wash a heart red, bringing a true belonging to the Father, a true security and foundation, and a true belonging to each other.

The blood of Jesus can unify the oldest with the youngest, the most intellectual and the unschooled, the richest and poorest, and those right across political divides. Because when you become family, real family, your new identity and condition supersede all of those things.

Presently the collective voice is shouting loudly, proclaiming a coming together of creeds and colors. The motive of the majority of concerned individuals cannot be criticized. But there is a deception here rooted in the spiritual realm. The solution is not conformity of peoples and cultures; neither is it a blind acceptance of contrasting aspects of them.

The solution is actually rooted in what someone has

already accomplished. New creations are the answer, not a manufactured gluing together of old ones.

So what of those slightly different "Christian" groups and organizations that appear to operate outside the mainstream churches?

5

CULTS—THE NEARLY MEN

A s with the previous chapter, we are not going to analyze every so-called cult; other available works have done so very well.

If there is a smorgasbord of religions, then there is equally one of so-called Christian organizations and groups who differ in belief from mainstream Christian, biblical premises and either strongly emphasize an element of choice or choose to ignore a particular tenet altogether.

For the purposes of the following comments, let's define a cult as a self-styled church, one in which a group or organization displaces Jesus Christ from His biblical position. We need to remember, as Jesus said, that not everyone who calls on His name is part of the church of Jesus Christ. Certain organizations would have us believe that they represent merely a different flavor of Christianity. Others are more explicit in their delineation concerning the Person of Jesus.

One example would be the Jehovah's Witnesses. Ignoring, for the moment, the way that the organization operates and the unease that has been expressed concerning its *modus operandi*, its stated theology denies that Jesus Christ is God. For our purposes, that makes it a cult.

Another would be the Mormon Church, also known as the Church of Jesus Christ of Latter-Day Saints. This organization accepts that Jesus was the Son of God but denies that He was God. He could attain God-ship through His life—as can we, say the Mormons; onto the cult pile, I'm afraid.

The Bible is our plumb line. I am all for diversity of expression of belief and worship; God would have His church to be an active powerhouse demonstrating signs and wonders; I readily welcome the gifts of the Holy Spirit and speaking in tongues, and I am a strong advocate for a dynamic, prophetic church! I acknowledge the ministry of angels and believe that we really can "go places" in the realm of prayer! Amen to the freedom of the Holy Spirit within us, through us, and among us corporately! May He been seen and witnessed in our church gatherings, in our homes, our workplaces, in coffee bars, nightclubs—everywhere!

But...

> For many deceivers have gone out into the world, those who do not acknowledge Jesus Christ as coming in the flesh. This is the deceiver and the antichrist.
>
> —2 JOHN 7

The key here is that many acknowledge that Jesus of Nazareth came in the flesh—He walked the earth. But to acknowledge that Jesus *Christ* came in the flesh, now that's a different matter altogether. And as Christians we assert the latter as well as the former!

Any spirit that tells me that Jesus is not the Messiah, is not the Son of God, or is not God Almighty can, with respect, go take a hike!

To deny the Person of Jesus is to deny the finished work

of the Cross. It denies the power of the blood of Jesus to reconcile us to the Father, denies the power of healing, and removes our authority to stand fast against the enemy. Jesus is the Lord of lords and King of kings. He is the undisputed champion of all that is seen and unseen.

You will not walk in the manifest presence of God if you deny who Jesus is, because in so doing you disqualify yourself from knowing Him. It is as we live in Him that He expresses Himself in and through us. What a privilege!

The Bible warns us that in the coming days, if it were possible, even those who consider themselves "rock solid" in the faith may be open to deception. Signs and wonders shine brightly; light attracts a whole variety of creatures to it. Not all light is His light. We need to maintain a close, intimate walk with Jesus to ensure that we continue safely on our walk with Him. It's true that nothing and no one can snatch us from His hands, but we want to ensure that our relationship with Him is as dear as it can be so as to avoid pitfalls planted by the enemy.

What emotions does the Cross of Jesus stir in you?

6

THE CROSS MEANS "WELCOME"

IN *FROM LEGAL to Regal* I shared the rather sad anecdote about a young woman who had decided to reject her Christian faith on the grounds that she simply could not dislodge her sense of guilt. She had turned to Islam since, she explained, that every time she looked at Jesus on the cross she felt guilty and that it was much simpler to follow a clear set of rules.

What a tragedy. The message of the Cross could not be more the opposite! The guiltless paid the price for the guilty, transferring His condition to the guilty party, redeeming us, and transforming us.

One mistake is that Christians tend to try very hard to live the Christian life. Understandably, they want to be successful and faithful. But, as my pastor says, "The Christian life is not difficult; it's *impossible!*" We just cannot live it in our own strength. We will fail again and again if we endeavor to live what is a walk of faith in the power of our own efforts and strivings.

As far as I can see, there is only *one* thing that the Bible tells us to strive for. And that is to remain in His rest! In His rest the Holy Spirit has our permission and the freedom to outwork the Life of Christ through us, negating the need for our own strivings. Only the indwelling Holy Spirit can manifest the Life of Christ in and through us. God designed this Life much more simply than we often-times have tried to exercise it.

Jesus did not die to improve us. He died so that we might *die* with Him and *be raised* in newness of Life. That's what being "born again" means. That's right; He died in order to *kill us*! How else could we embrace newness of Life if we continued to live from our old nature? This kind of spiritual schizophrenia is exhausting and not how God designed us to function.

Schizophrenia is an illness "in which people have difficulties in their thought processes leading to hallucinations, delusions, disordered thinking and unusual speech or behaviour."[1] Maybe not in a literal sense, but too many believers seem to manifest such disorders spiritually.

Please do not misunderstand me; I am not criticizing any of us. I am only too well aware of the battles and of the struggles I have walked through myself. Indeed, it is only because I have walked through (perhaps "crawled" and "prayed" through would be more accurate at times!) delusions and disordered thinking myself that I am in a position to write with the aim of sharing that there is freedom in Christ Jesus!

For reasons that I will not go into here, I walked in considerable guilt for many years. Oh, I knew the theology. I knew that Jesus had died and risen to take me as His own and to bring me into freedom. But I was blind in areas, which meant I could not receive His goodness in the core of who I was.

Do you know that it is the *kindness* of the Lord that leads us to repentance (to change) (Rom. 2:4)? In Jesus, God is now your Father, a perfect father who knows you intimately and has decided, of His own free will, to love you, to unconditionally accept you, to walk with you, to develop you, and to mature you, all of which brings freedom as its fruit. In Jesus you are not going to experience the wrath of His nature because His wrath is only shown where injustice perpetuates. It's a kind of jealousy for justice, if you like. Hence, you will not experience or be subject to it, because justice has been satisfied on your account. Your sins and failures are no longer in the heavenly record; they were washed away two thousand years ago on the Cross of Jesus.

If you have never received Jesus as your own, personal Lord and Savior, have a look please at the back of the book; there's an appendix there to guide you through to do just that. It's not complicated. He is eagerly waiting to introduce Himself to you!

As Christians, this fact of our new condition needs to go deep into the core of how we live from our new identity, so I would like to say it again: All your sins and failures, be they past, present or future, have been cleansed in the blood of Jesus. God does not look at you with love from one eye and with judgment from the other. So, when we struggle in areas of our lives, we can come to Him *in those things* and know that we will not be rejected in any sense, nor will we be sneered at or disrespected. He is kind, and as He reveals His nature to us, we change; we are touched from within and sprout new fruit. When He does such a real, lasting, and genuine work of transformation in us, we hardly know how to explain the changes that occur in us. Others may ask you for the formula (everyone wants a quick fix if it's available), but you will simply be able to point them to Jesus, the author and finisher of your faith. You will realize that, somehow, God loved you into transformation.

I feel awful for the girl who turned to Islam; following a set of rules may seem to offer security, but there is no Holy Spirit Life outside of the Cross, and none of the wonderful fruits that He works in us—love, joy, peace, patience, and many others. She has tied herself to a life of strife, self-judgment, and perpetual self-monitoring. Placing her faith in an ability to keep rules, she will hope that somehow this distant God will consider her efforts sufficient for her to be acceptable to Him.

I pray that the Lord reveals Himself to her. May she meet the One who can set her free from a life of such toil.

Life is available to her, to you, and to me.

7

RESURRECTION AND LIFE

FOLLOWING THE EVENT of the crucifixion, Jesus died and remained busy. He went into hell and effected the most significant raid in eternal history. He took back the authority that Adam had yielded in the Garden of Eden. Taking back the keys to the gates of hell (*gates* signify a place of authority; city gates were places where decisions were taken by elders) meant that Satan would no longer have lasting dominion, or the final word on the destination of men's souls. Each individual now had the regained right to choose their eternal destination.

For those who have aligned themselves with the finished work of the Cross, the divine exchange we have referred to does not only involve the complete transfer of sin and legal guilt to Jesus but also the transfer of His Life and nature to us.

We have been crucified with Christ, but we have not expired. Our old nature has been put to death and we have received a new nature—our spirit man "made alive" by the indwelling Spirit of God. The following scripture ought to dazzle us if we are really hearing what it is saying: "This spirit is the same spirit that raised Christ from the dead..." (Romans 8:11)

Excuse me? The same spirit! The Bible could not be plainer, could it? The Spirit that raised Jesus from the dead is the same one that lives in us as Christians. We have been made alive, and we have been made sons. Royal sons.

It is little wonder that the enemy seeks to cause us to doubt our identity in Jesus. It is worth taking a look, once in a while, at the nature and flavor of some of the struggles we go through. Often the nature of their agenda is set to discourage us from standing firm in the Life of Christ. Our enemy is *very* jealous of us; that's for sure.

MOVING IN OPPOSITE DIRECTIONS

While Satan once enjoyed a lofty position in the exalted vaults of heaven and has since been cast down, we, once distanced from the glory of Father's presence, have been brought near.

Satan was an angel, a being of beauty. He has been irredeemably cast out of heaven and knows that we are citizens of that same place. It isn't as if we deserved it, is it? Alienated from God, the sacrifice of another paid for our release and enabled us to become citizens of the very realm where Lucifer once shone in beauty.

It is sometimes hard for us to respond to the grace of God. We are so used to having to *earn* acceptance that to be *given* it, dare I say it, so outrageously takes a genuine humility for us to admit our need and to express our gratitude, saying, "Yes, please. Thank you." Then, having been acquitted from the court and of all charges against our name, we discover that our Redeemer has set us up for our future. He has set us up for Life. We find out that we are on an amazing path of discovery as the Holy Spirit, the revelator, begins to unpack the undeserved, incredible provision that has been made for us ex-prisoners. Not only are the prisoners pardoned, but also they are adopted. Not only are they adopted and given the full provision and inheritance of sons, but also their very *nature* is renewed.

One of the most common discussions around the value of incarcerating criminals concerns the role of rehabilitation. A Christian website comments:

> One day a Christian and a Communist were sitting on a park bench watching the world go by. As they watched, a poor, drunken beggar walked by dressed in rags. The Communist pointed to the beggar and said, "Communism would put a new suit on that man!" To which the Christian responded, "Maybe so, but Jesus Christ can put a new man in that suit."[1]

Jesus actually supplies us with a new nature. As we receive revelation that this has already taken place, we begin to live from a place of rest, which allows that nature to express itself.

In Jesus we are not required to strive to produce His nature. He has already given us a new nature. In His rest it will grow and cause us to grow up in Him.

"It is finished!" Can our faith partner with that exclamation?

8

THE FINAL ANSWER AND THE MASS

FOR US TO truly live in the reality of Jesus's completion of our redemption and transfer out of death and into Christ's Life, we have to be clear about what happened at the Cross and also about what didn't happen. Speaking of Jewish ritual, Paul says of the Mosaic Law in Hebrews:

> For the Law, since it has only a shadow of the good things to come and not the very form of things, can never, by the same sacrifices which they offer continually year by year, make perfect those who draw near. Otherwise, would they not have ceased to be offered, because the worshipers, having once been cleansed, would no longer have had consciousness of sins?
> —HEBREWS 10:1–2

The New Living Translation puts verse 1 like this:

> The old system under the law of Moses was only a shadow, a dim preview of the good things to come, not the good things themselves. The sacrifices under that system were repeated again and again, year after year, but they were never able to provide perfect cleansing for those who came to worship.

The Message Bible says:

> The old plan was only a hint of the good things in the new plan. Since that old "law plan" wasn't complete in itself, it couldn't complete those who followed it. No matter how many sacrifices were offered year after year, they never added up to a complete solution.

While the repeated sacrifices stipulated in the Law were ineffective in bringing about a "complete solution," what, in contrast, did Jesus do?

> For by one offering He has perfected for all time those who are sanctified.
>
> —Hebrews 10:14

The J. B. Phillips New Testament puts the verse like this:

> For by virtue of that one offering he has perfected for all time every one whom he makes holy.

I like that. In Jesus Christ we *have been* perfected for all time. How glorious! It is not dependent upon our weekly performance, sense of spirituality, or good works (as welcome as good works are). He has done it *all* for all time.

Unless we come to a place of rest in that finished work, our desire for intimacy with God will always be frustrated. If we strive to be accepted by Jesus, we will never arrive at the sheltered port called Rest.

Check Your Bag Again

Have you ever searched high and low for something you thought you had mislaid, only to find it in your pocket?

It is illogical to spend our lives striving for something we already have. As children laugh at a clown who makes a play of looking for a piece of paper that he has stuck to his forehead, so many believers are looking for something they have already been given. I am not suggesting that these dear Christians are to be mocked; on the contrary, my desire is for us all to see what was achieved at the Cross and to embrace it.

In Christ we have been given His peace. We have been given His forgiveness and His acceptance. How long are we going to continue to sweep the room that has already been cleansed? I suppose we will do that until the veil falls from our spiritual eyes.

Might we dare to believe just how good this Good News is?

MASS AND HOLY COMMUNION

Jesus had a meal with His disciples prior to His Passion; I believe that it was much more about fellowship together than it was about instituting some form of church "rite":

> For I received from the Lord that which I also delivered to you, that the Lord Jesus in the night in which He was betrayed took bread; and when He had given thanks, He broke it and said, "This is My body, which is for you; do this in remembrance of Me." In the same way He took the cup also after supper, saying, "This cup is the new covenant in My blood; do this, as often as you drink it, in remembrance of Me." For as often as you eat this bread and drink the cup, you proclaim the Lord's death until He comes.
>
> —1 CORINTHIANS 11:23–26

This intimacy was going to be made possible because Jesus was about to complete His mission of reconciling us back to the Father. This was going to provide a solid, immovable foundation in our lives, not some kind of vague, flimsy hope that the Father might be feeling benevolent toward us.

Believers celebrate and participate in Holy Communion (also known as the Lord's Supper) in regular church services as well as at other times. "In remembrance of Me…": families and friends share emblems in their homes or even remember Him together over a meal.

The idea, therefore, that participation in Holy Communion may not serve as a wonderful reminder of what Jesus has accomplished for us is, frankly, a travesty. We come to the table *thankful* that we have been forgiven, not begging for what we already have. This is not a time to remember what we have done wrong; rather, it is to acknowledge what He did right! As we "examine" ourselves (1 Cor. 11:28), we joyfully are reminded that we stand guiltless in His presence. We don't need to navel gaze but rather Savior gaze!

Comparing the Scriptures concerning the Jewish law and the finished work of the Cross bring the Catholic Mass, therefore, into a clearer definition.

Regardless of how the congregations of Catholics approach their participation in what the Catholic Church calls "The Mass," official church teaching holds that the symbolic bread and wine, once blessed, become *in essence* the body and blood of Jesus. This simply cannot be true.

In Hebrews 7 we read of Jesus:

> For it was fitting for us to have such a high priest…who does not need daily, like those high

> priests, to offer up sacrifices, first for His own sins
> and then for the sins of the people, *because this He
> did once for all when He offered up Himself.*
> —HEBREWS 7:26–27, EMPHASIS ADDED

The Message reads:

> He's done it, once and for all: offered up himself as
> the sacrifice.

If the bread and wine were being literally transformed, then Jesus did not die *once*. Scripture clearly states that He did.

The wonder of "once for all" is that we all have the opportunity to embrace His sacrifice and to come to a place of glorious rest in it. There is nothing more to add. It is a finished work, one that does not need to be repeated.

One that never will be repeated. Hallelujah!

Our old nature recognized the concept of shame very well. If we believe that the work of the Cross is unfinished, our shame remains. We would approach God unsure of our position at best and plagued by guilt at worst. There is no resting place in living life in this way.

Our shame has been removed because Jesus was shamed, once and for all, for us. This releases us into a glorious place of rest. His blood truly births glory into our lives!

9

THE POWER OF THE CROSS IN MUSIC

USIC PLAYS A central role in much of our Christian worship. Indeed, there is an extensive range
of excellent material available that can stir in
us the desire to worship the Lord and accompany some
of our intimate moments with Him. Up-to-date recording
and production methods ensure that not only the musicianship but also the precious anointing of the Spirit can
be "captured" magnificently. I think that musicianship is
now, quite regularly, of the highest quality, unsurpassed
probably in the history of the Christian music industry.

If you enjoy contemporary worship, you are probably
familiar with many of those worshipping musicians who
are helping us to encounter God in music: Bethel Church in
Redding, California; MorningStar Ministries in Charlotte,
North Carolina; Jesus Culture; a broad catalog from the
Vineyard—we really are spoiled these days. In addition,
"soaking" music is now widely available through musicans
such as Alberto and Kimberly Rivera. Soaking music that
carries an anointing is like taking a bath in the Holy Spirit;
just let the water and the gentle suds cover you, cleanse you,
and touch you at your core as you yield to Him.

Moreover, the anointing on much of this music is also

being "bottled" and distributed to anyone with an MP3 player and CD player. The Holy Spirit is inhabiting music to touch and bring healing and release to listeners all over the world on an unprecedented scale.

Video and web streaming, now so readily available to millions across the globe, ensure that the extra visual dimension can almost instantly bless multitudes. A powerful night of worship captured even on a mobile phone may be viewed freely within minutes on websites such as YouTube. As technology and excellence have expanded their lines of influence, so the world's borders continue to shrink. News spreads so fast today, of course. God moves in a place, and media such as Twitter and Facebook inform you almost before the event has occurred!

Not that all Christian music is necessarily anointed, if I may so. The anointing tends to emanate from those who walk closely with Jesus; it is much more than seeking to make a great record. I concede that there is an element of subjectivity, of course. Why shouldn't the Holy Spirit wing blessing to you through music that may actually leave me untouched? He is not limited, is He?

As a worship leader I prefer to be careful not to assume that all worship involves music! It plainly does not. There are countless ways, both artistic and otherwise, to offer Him worship. We may worship Him with our voices or silently. Making someone a cup of coffee can be an act of worship, as could a genuine smile of encouragement. I do think that the Word of God in music is very powerful, as is heartfelt declaration of love for our Savior.

I have met those whom the Holy Spirit has touched very deeply through secular music too. He is not limited in how He works, that's for sure. I am sure that on many an occasion, lyrics that were originally intended to be sung as a love song to a person have been hijacked by the Holy Spirit to touch someone deeply. Well, He has the right, don't you think?

There are also seasons for the anointing moving upon, in, and through us in different ways. Have you found that to be the case? This is certainly true of the anointing on music too. I can recall songs that, for a season, spoke powerfully and through which the Holy Spirit ministered strongly, both to me personally and also in the local and wider church. It's important to discern the anointing; otherwise we can make the mistake of continuing in what God may have lifted His hand from. Just because it was right or anointed before does not mean that it is now. We need to stay "current" with the Holy Spirit. He does not particularly like formulas!

When we have a revelation of the Cross, some of the old hymns take on new life! I remember my first Christmas as a born-again believer. I was thrilled to sing the words of some of the traditional carols! They had taken on a new dimension. I can't say that "Little Donkey" especially grabbed my spirit (apologies to whoever wrote that particular one!), but how about these words from Charles Wesley's "Hark! The Herald Angels Sing"?

> Peace on earth and mercy mild,
> God and sinners reconciled…
>
> Veiled in flesh the Godhead see;
> Hail the incarnate Deity!…
>
> Born to raise the sons of earth,
> Born to give them second birth.[1]

Hail the incarnate deity! Amen! Jesus is equally Deity, as is Father and the Holy Spirit.

When you read the words of some of the old hymns, my goodness, they are powerful, and you sense that the original download from God must have been truly significant, one full of revelation.

Here is another one of my favorites! These words are from Elisha A. Hoffman's "Are You Washed in the Blood?"

> Have you been to Jesus for the cleansing pow'r?
> Are you washed in the blood of the Lamb?
> Are you fully trusting in His grace this hour?
> Are you washed in the blood of the Lamb?
>
> Are you washed in the blood, in the soul-cleaning
>   blood of the Lamb?
> Are your garments spotless?
> Are they white as snow?
> Are you washed in the blood of the Lamb?[2]

I love to see the Gospel in those words. We can read and sing of what Jesus did for us on the cross. This grace that is freely ours, is ours for all eternity. It is good to consider His imminent return and of the reality of heaven, where there will be no more pain and suffering, no more tears; a place where there will only be joy, genuine joy, the kind that springs from the presence of God and satisfies us in the deepest recesses of our hearts.

Have you noticed that many worship ministries, including some of those that have been on the cutting edge of new, expansive, and prophetic expressions of worship in music, have at times taken hold of an old hymn as the vehicle of anointing, perhaps setting the song slightly differently?

And there are times when the music flows in the anointing, we don't even know what words to sing. Perhaps there are no words…just sounds—sounds of longing, of love, of yearning, of celebration, of intercession. The Spirit joins us and kingdom is established!

The Holy Spirit wants to tutor us; He wants to lead our worship, partnering with us so that in the manifest presence of God, kingdom values and kingdom authority may be established here where we are, on earth. Our physical bodies may be here in this world, but we are spiritually alive and operate from heavenly places. You and I have been seated there with Christ. I believe that from that place God wants to sing over us; He wants us to hear the sounds of heaven so that we may transmit them on earth. God wants the earth to hear the sounds of heaven! We may or may not get goose bumps in His presence, but His goal is to affect our realm here. This happens as we honor the Person of the Holy Spirit. He presences Himself with a kingdom agenda.

He is not going to move freely if we try to manipulate Him and conform Him to an agenda of our own. The manifestation of the kingdom of God is possible in our gatherings, our homes, and, in fact, wherever we are as carriers of His presence.

This kind of manifestation only comes through the Cross. It is the Cross that has transferred us from darkness to light. It is through the Cross that we have been reconciled to God and into intimacy with Him. We worship Him in spirit, primarily. Should it be any surprise that God's children, who are seated in heavenly places, should be able to hear the sounds of heaven? As we do so, we can be vessels of His glory, transmitters of the glory, people filled with His Spirit, able to hear and reproduce heaven's music.

God created the earth with a sound. He spoke and it was. He said "Light!" and it *was*. It *wasn't* and then it *was*! His voice, His very sound has creative possibilities. He is so awesome. I believe the days are fast approaching when a simple, even single sound heard from heaven will contain the glory of God and break strongholds here on earth—strongholds of infirmity, of bondage, of confusion.

These walls are going to fall, people!

Worship is a spiritual deal! Worship is about Him first and foremost. We want to glorify Him; to glorify means to acknowledge and "allow to be seen." He is already full of glory, but He wants us to partner with Him and facilitate the revealing of Him on earth.

As a worship leader myself, a great compliment you could give me after a time of musical worship might be your silence; that you and I might be so awestruck by the sense of His presence; that we might be captivated by Him and therefore be walking "glory people," spreading kingdom favor everywhere we go.

It's great if you enjoyed this or that song, but we are no longer satisfied with a decent band, excellent sound, talent, and original material. All those things are indeed excellent, and there is nothing wrong with wanting excellence. But, oh my goodness, when His presence is among us and the body is filled, enthused and demonstrating kingdom and healing of all kinds is taking place spontaneously during our times of worship, now that's the direction we need to be heading in.

I remember being in a meeting some years ago. After our customary time of extravagant worship (we sure had some amazing times of worship in the presence of God in the fellowship I was part of at that time), this missionary lady who had been invited stepped up to minister. She, as

I remember, had seen much of the supernatural activity of God where she was stationed (where, I do not remember).

Before speaking, she said that she wanted us to worship the Lord together. She took out what looked like a home-made instrument; it looked like a shoebox with strings. I remember rather disdaining it in my heart; it didn't look very modern—on the contrary, it seemed to be archaic! I imagined this was going to be embarrassing, a weak episode, and I judged her inwardly as I prepared to "tolerate" her singing, or worshipping, with such a primitive-looking contraption.

She started to sing. She began to worship. Her voice was tender, not forceful. She ran her fingers through the strings and, as if playing a harp, accompanied her sung words.

Here's the thing. The anointing was rich. She was worshipping with a "shoebox," and I sat there undone, struck by the gentle presence of God that invaded as she ministered. Because *that* is what she intended to do; her desire was to minister to Jesus. He showed that He really enjoyed it by drawing close to listen *well*! My attitude stank, to be truthful, but He didn't condemn me. His love touched me, and, as I say, my judgment was undone in His presence.

I love to pray for worship leaders. My desire for them is that they will, first and foremost, be worshippers; that they will encounter Him in intimacy; that they will operate in the prophetic, sounding out heaven's divine order through their music.

Of course this is not just for them alone; we are all worshippers, welcome in the holy place, friends of God in Christ Jesus, sons who have a destiny to impact the earth with expressions of the finished work of the Cross.

10

THE GLORY, PART 1

TAKE A BRIEF trip with me into Leviticus. It may not be the most-oft visited book of the Bible in terms of everyday reading. Oh, but the Holy Spirit knows how to open up some gems to us, ones that, if we can catch them in our spirits, may dramatically impact our faith walk and its outworking in our lives. Leviticus 9 could be such a passage, one that can light a fire in us and transform our sense of self-esteem as we realize the awesome power of the Cross in our lives.

Jesus said that man does not live by bread alone but by every word that comes from God's mouth. The most significant changes I have known take place in my life have been due to a revelation from the Holy Spirit that I have been able to "own" as my own. That's how I appropriate it. I say, "This is for me, for Steve. It's paid for, it's been delivered to me, so I say 'Yes, thank you,'" and I receive it.

Below is Leviticus 9 in full. Try not to skip any of it or rush through it. Allow the Holy Spirit to deposit something in you as you read. You may not even know what that is yet, but the Word is living and active, especially when it is winged into our hearts supernaturally.

Now it came about on the eighth day that Moses called Aaron and his sons and the elders of Israel; and he said to Aaron, "Take for yourself a calf, a bull, for a sin offering and a ram for a burnt offering, both without defect, and offer them before the LORD. Then to the sons of Israel you shall speak, saying, 'Take a male goat for a sin offering, and a calf and a lamb, both one year old, without defect, for a burnt offering, and an ox and a ram for peace offerings, to sacrifice before the LORD, and a grain offering mixed with oil; for today the LORD will appear to you.'" So they took what Moses had commanded to the front of the tent of meeting, and the whole congregation came near and stood before the LORD. Moses said, "This is the thing which the LORD has commanded you to do, that the glory of the LORD may appear to you." Moses then said to Aaron, "Come near to the altar and offer your sin offering and your burnt offering, that you may make atonement for yourself and for the people; then make the offering for the people, that you may make atonement for them, just as the LORD has commanded."

So Aaron came near to the altar and slaughtered the calf of the sin offering which was for himself. Aaron's sons presented the blood to him; and he dipped his finger in the blood and put *some* on the horns of the altar, and poured out the rest of the blood at the base of the altar. The fat and the kidneys and the lobe of the liver of the sin offering, he then offered up in smoke on the altar just as the LORD had commanded Moses. The flesh and the skin, however, he burned with fire outside the camp.

Then he slaughtered the burnt offering; and Aaron's sons handed the blood to him and he sprinkled it around on the altar. They handed the burnt offering to him in pieces, with the head, and he offered them up in smoke on the altar. He also washed the entrails and the legs, and offered them up in smoke with the burnt offering on the altar.

Then he presented the people's offering, and took the goat of the sin offering which was for the people, and slaughtered it and offered it for sin, like the first. He also presented the burnt offering, and offered it according to the ordinance. Next he presented the grain offering, and filled his hand with some of it and offered it up in smoke on the altar, besides the burnt offering of the morning.

Then he slaughtered the ox and the ram, the sacrifice of peace offerings which was for the people; and Aaron's sons handed the blood to him and he sprinkled it around on the altar. As for the portions of fat from the ox and from the ram, the fat tail, and the fat covering, and the kidneys and the lobe of the liver, they now placed the portions of fat on the breasts; and he offered them up in smoke on the altar. But the breasts and the right thigh Aaron presented as a wave offering before the LORD, just as Moses had commanded.

Then Aaron lifted up his hands toward the people and blessed them, and he stepped down after making the sin offering and the burnt offering and the peace offerings. Moses and Aaron went into the tent of meeting. When they came out and blessed the people, the glory of the LORD appeared to all the people. Then fire came out from before the LORD and consumed the burnt offering and the portions of fat on the altar; and when all the people saw it, they shouted and fell on their faces.

Remember, I am no theologian and do not wish to try to share as one. I can only share how the Holy Spirit and His Word impact me!

This chapter is a sensational read! Five animals are slaughtered on the sacrificial altar. The detail is impressive. In verse 4 we read that Moses tells Aaron that through these rituals the Lord is "going to appear to him." What a stunning promise! In verse 6 Moses tells him again, but he puts it differently. The glory of the Lord is going to appear, he foretells.

As the process continues, there is evidently a lot of blood. *A lot* of blood. Blood is sprinkled all over the altar. We considered this in chapter 1. I do respectfully wonder how you would even start to go about cleaning up that lot.

As the priests bless the people who are watching the ceremony, the glory of the Lord appears. I read this and want to ask the Lord, "So, Lord, what did that look like exactly?" Was it light? Dazzling light? Did they physically see the glory, or was it more a perception of something awesome taking place spiritually? I imagine that the visual presence of the glory of God had a lot to do with Moses and Aaron, as it was when they appeared before the people, blessing them, that the glory was seen. All the people saw His glory. A ceremony filled with the sacrificial blood of five animals, performed with a genuine, right heart had attracted such a presence of God that the Bible says that all the people saw God's glory.

And then, if that wasn't enough, fire came. Fire. Real fire. Flames. Fire burned up the offerings on the altar. It must have been, in a sense, terrifying. The people fell on their faces with a shout, the chapter concludes.

God's glory was associated with His holiness, with His displays, at times, of devastating power. It was associated with fear and terror. The people did not know Him. They knew of His deeds; they had seen miraculous deeds themselves, deeds of deliverance and of punishment. This God was unapproachable. Though the people did not have, in the main, a sense of personal relationship with Him, yet they knew that He was their God; they usually needed Him to be their God the most when they had distanced themselves from Him through their frequent and regular disobedience. He was still the God of Abraham, Isaac, and Jacob.

God's glory reminded the people of their sinful nature and behavior. It was only through blood, the shedding of much blood, that they were in a position to walk as His people.

In Jesus Christ the picture is transformed. With a new nature birthed inside of us, with a new position in the spiritual realm, having received glory from Jesus as we abide in Him, gifted with a new identity, the glory of God now becomes an environment to participate in and cherish. That is not to say that it is in any sense less awesome. Indeed, is it not more awesome still that people such as us have been brought near by the blood of Jesus, brought near to the glory? This is something to be revered, honored, and rightly feared.

11

THE GLORY, PART 2

O N OTHER OCCASIONS in the Bible we read that vast numbers of animals were slaughtered in sacrifices at festivals, celebrations, and at feasts. On one such occasion 22,000 bulls are sacrificed together with 120,000 sheep.

Can we even begin to fathom what that might have looked like? If, as we read in Leviticus 9, the sacrifice of five animals resulted in a blood-soaked chamber, where does our imagination even begin to go with numbers such as these?

The question pounding my senses is this: *Just how important is blood?*

The regulations handed down to men via appointed ministers such as Moses and Aaron were that these sacrifices were to be made to atone for the people. There would have been gallons and gallons of blood.

Apparently there are about 45 liters of blood in your average cow. Notwithstanding that the whole quantity from each animal would not have spilled, the slaughter of 22,000 bulls would equate to something in the region of 990,000 liters or 218,000 gallons of blood. An Olympic swimming pool holds about 2,500,000 liters, so that gives you an idea.

That's before we even count the sheep!

In Leviticus 11 God explains that the life is in the blood. Blood had to be shed to deal with the penalty of sin. Without the shedding of blood there was no forgiveness.

The New Testament is not ambiguous about the precious nature of the blood of Christ.

> But now in Christ Jesus you who formerly were far
> off have been brought near by the blood of Christ.
> —EPHESIANS 2:13

The J. B. Phillips New Testament translation quotes verses 11 to 13 as follows:

> Do not lose sight of the fact that you were born "Gentiles", known by those whose bodies were circumcised as "the uncircumcised". You were without Christ, you were utter strangers to God's chosen community, the Jews, and you had no knowledge of, or right to, the promised agreements. You had nothing to look forward to and no God to whom you could turn. But now, through the blood of Christ, you who were once outside the pale are with us inside the circle of God's love and purpose.

Jesus—His nature, death, and resurrection are the cornerstone of our faith. Our entire relationship with Him is due to who He is and what He has done for us. And this work that He has started in us and promises to continue stands on the same foundation. Ransomed sinners have become sons, and many "religious sons," those who for a multitude of reasons have struggled with the bondages of legalism and religion, are finding freedom in Christ. They are discovering the glories of a supernatural life walk with Jesus where the kingdom of Heaven expresses itself. As

Jesus glorified the Father, the Father glorified Him. As we live in Him, the glory lives in and through us.

There is no glory apart from the blood of Jesus. Apart from His blood, a form of "church" could continue, religion could thrive, movements could come and go, but the glory that is being revealed and going to be revealed through the church of Jesus Christ is inseparable from His blood. In Him we live and move and have our being (Acts 17:28). Our life "moves"—it is fluid in Jesus, crucified and risen. We were crucified with Christ, and when He rose, so did we. Our life is in Him, our life in the kingdom is His Life.

Any attempts to shift the centrality of who Jesus is and what He has done for us will, for those who may do so, derail the move of God's presence in their lives. God's presence in us is going to reveal the glorious Christ in and through the church. These end days are going to culminate in the evidenced reality of a glorious Husband and bride.

She is His glory; He has given His glory to her, and she seeks to glorify the glorified Husband. This kind of unity is unbreakable. No wonder the church is described as an army, terrible with banners (Song of Sol. 6). She is the church who is not only passionate about the centrality of the Cross but also bold to boast in it. Though the Cross may be an offensive message to some, the bride's love for her Husband far supersedes her concerns about any disgruntled opposition.

We may remind ourselves that our King is not like us. He is far more generous than we are. He is far more extravagant. He expresses His nature through us, that is true. We desire to bless and to give because we have experienced His nature, and that same nature desires to reign in us. We have to unlearn so much of the *modus operandi* of our former lives: the need to look after our own interests first and our attempts to shore up our positions and guarantee our security.

The King of kings is all glorious. He is rich, full of joy, a warm, vibrant personality. He delights in us and delights in our progress. As we live in the Spirit, we are able, we are liberated to delight in others' progress and blessings.

GOLD DUST—WHY NOT?

I have been in meetings when the gold dust appeared! I have been in the presence of the miraculous. Should we expect any less when the King is among us?

You may or may not experience the gold dust, feathers in the air, the holy presence of angels, and other manifestations such as these. I rejoice with you if you do. The King is a liberal benefactor. Permit me to give you my take on such things.

The King enjoys doing it. Ha ha!

Perhaps we forget, at times, that He does not have to explain Himself. Not even *we* feel obliged to do that, as a matter of course, much less so, then, *Him*. If we, made in His image, enjoy blessing others just for the sake of it, why would He be any less lavish?

We really have much to learn about the nature of our God, Father, and King. But that's all right. Let's just press on in Him from where we are. He is with us; He started it all and is committed to revealing ever more of Himself to us and through us! Glory in the church!

His glory feeds and clothes us, provides our needs, He gives us work, shelters, and families to be part of. He gives us humor and fun, unexpected gifts and surprises.

The world may still be a fallen one, but *the King is about His royal business* and discharging not only responsibilities but also gifts to His regal princes and princesses.

12

BLOOD—A SPIRITUAL ISSUE

THE HEAVENLY REALMS know about the power of the blood of Jesus.

But you have come to Mount Zion and to the city of the living God, the heavenly Jerusalem, and to myriads of angels, to the general assembly and church of the firstborn who are enrolled in heaven, and to God, the Judge of all, and to the spirits of the righteous made perfect, and to Jesus, the mediator of a new covenant, and to the sprinkled blood, *which speaks better* than the blood of Abel.
—HEBREWS 12:22–24, EMPHASIS ADDED

In Genesis God said that Abel's blood cried out to Him from the earth. Abel had been murdered by his brother, Cain. Blood was shed, and God *heard the blood.*

Scripture says a lot about blood. We have seen that it tells us that life is in the blood. It says that the blood of bulls and goats cannot take away sins. It says that only the unique, spotless, sin-free blood of Jesus has the power to do that.

Since time immemorial men have shed blood in an expectation to gain power, to gain position, to appease "gods," and to seek the favor of such "gods." There is something in the DNA of man that knows that blood is hugely significant. I am always interested to read of the place and honor given to blood in religions. Religions can never bring us to God. But the deep, deep heart's desire of man is to be reconciled with his Creator. In ignorance, he seeks this by the shedding of blood.

The following is taken from a BBC report from 2004:

> The streets of Dhaka are ready to run red with blood.
>
> It can only mean one thing—Eid ul Adha, Islam's annual festival of sacrifice is here.
>
> But Sadiq Hossain, the mayor of the Bangladeshi capital, wants this year to be different.
>
> Hundreds of thousands of cattle will be sacrificed in the capital and across Bangladesh on 2 February.
>
> Mr Hossain is urging those who can to carry out the sacrifice in public parks.
>
> But he knows that in this crowded city most animals will be slaughtered in the street, leaving the stench of blood hanging in the air for days....
>
> Verses from the Koran are recited before the cattle are despatched [sic] with a sword across the throat.[1]

Similarly, to mark the Islamic festival of Ashura, Shiite pilgrims strike themselves, often self- flagellating with sharp objects such as swords, razors, and knives. One report has described the scene as one of "free-flowing blood...like a movie-scene massacre."[2]

A Hindu festival also involves sacrifice and the shedding of blood:

> Held at the same time as Raksha Bandhan, the Hindu festival observed by brothers and sisters

in honor of their relationship, a two-day festival is observed in the small Himalayan town of Devi Dhura in Uttar Pradesh, India. Hindus gather at the shrine of Varahi Devi or Bhagwati, an incarnation of Durga. She is the patron goddess of the approximately 200 villages in the area. Animal sacrifices—originally male buffaloes, but often bulls or goats today—are made at the shrine on the day before Raksha Bandhan. Processions from the other villages stream in to Devi Dhura. Generally these are led by dancers, followed by the animals, the priest, and members of the community. As hundreds of goats and bulls are killed, people use the blood to mark their foreheads.[3]

You get the picture; we could add descriptions too from the African continent and others. The notion of sacrifice as an act of worship is a worldwide one. This is because it is widely understood in the spiritual realms.

The Lamb of God, Jesus Christ the Son, was slain from the foundation of the world. Only in God's wondrous economy and eternal reality could the pieces all fit together.

Before a sin had been committed, before a man had been formed (let alone breathed), heaven saw the complete, unveiled future and ensured that man, God's creation, would not remain separated from home. The fruit had not yet been tasted in Eden, including "that" particular piece of fruit. In His supreme foreknowledge, the Trinity of God arranged redemption. God knew when the time would be right.

> For while we were still helpless, *at the right time* Christ died for the ungodly.
> —ROMANS 5:6, EMPHASIS ADDED

God saw the swathes of humanity who would be born in sin nature and made a way. His own arm took action in the absence of any other savior. Only pure, undefiled, unspoiled blood could effectively substitute in sacrifice. Only One could meet that requirement. Only One could be born of untainted blood, through a Holy Spirit conception. Only His blood would do.

It is as if the whole of creation knows intrinsically that there is something precious, something fearful, something noble about blood. Woven deeply into our psyche is the understanding that we are in need of redemption, in need of reconciliation, in need of rescuing. Events that issue from our lives and from national and international society around us only serve to confirm it.

It isn't as if men do not try to get along, and try to find God too. They make great efforts in diverse ways. But we have to keep in mind that there is a spiritual dimension operating all the time. While men strive for reconciliation with each other through dialogue and conferences, blogs, and interfaith, frustration results time and time again. It is like trying to walk in one direction when a magnet is ever drawing you in the opposite. Men know what they need but see their powerlessness to achieve it.

So hope is placed in committees and working groups and in strenuous efforts to find the common ground. Well, there is a common ground. It's called sin nature.

Equally, the other common ground is that there is only one means of disarming that nature and seeing it overcome by a greater nature. An eternal nature.

Just think about that for a moment. It really does us the power of good to acknowledge our inestimable value and how precious we are to God. He loved us so much that He gave Jesus as a substitute sacrifice, that anyone who would accept this holy work on his own account (my account, your account) would be credited with the righteousness of the one sacrificed. Dear God, we can never repay You. We can only say "Thank You" from the bottom of our hearts.

Having accepted this holy sacrifice on our own behalf, the Bible tells us that we now have a different identity:

> In Him, you also, after listening to the message of truth, the gospel of your salvation—having also believed, you were *sealed* in Him with the Holy Spirit of promise.
>
> —EPHESIANS 1:13, EMPHASIS ADDED

You have a spiritual seal. A seal is defined as "an emblem of authentication." Come on! You are authentically redeemed in Christ Jesus, not because of anything you have done but because you recognize that it is by His blood alone that you have been drawn near, back into relationship with Him.

A seal is also a device for ensuring that locked contents are not tampered with. Historically, important letters or communiqués were sealed with a seal of authority, perhaps in wax or a similar material.[4] We are so secure in Christ; we cannot be tampered with. The gold is inside us—His life, His nature.

It—and we—are going to endure and thrive for all eternity.

13

DECLARING PRAYER

I WOULD LIKE TO share something about prayer.

> Therefore, we are ambassadors for Christ, as though God were making an appeal through us; we beg you on behalf of Christ, be reconciled to God.
>
> —2 CORINTHIANS 5:20

Wikipedia defines *ambassador* as follows:

> An ambassador is an official envoy; especially, a highest ranking diplomat who represents a State and is usually accredited to another sovereign State (country), or to an international organization as the resident representative of his or her own government or sovereign or appointed for a special and often temporary diplomatic assignment.[1]

If you are thinking that you did not apply for such a lofty position, please understand that it comes with kingdom territory. You and I are now His ambassadors; we carry His authority. The kingdom of God is absolutely an international organization, and we certainly have a diplomatic assignment.

Not that we are to negotiate with darkness. We have

authority to dispel it with the light that is Christ in us, the hope of glory.

When we have a revelation of the Cross, we pray differently. We forsake the "if it be Your will, Lord" prayers and pray from the Word of God "made alive" ("breathed") in us and through the Holy Spirit in us. The Holy Spirit will never have us pray contrary to the Word of God. As we have revelation of who we are in Christ and of our inheritance, we exercise that authority in declaration. We decree in His name.

I think of it like a set of traffic lights. I exercise my authority in Christ to turn the light "red" if an anti-Christ agenda is seeking to hold sway. I turn the light to "green" when I decree the way of the kingdom. A green light says, "Yes! Full steam ahead! Let kingdom order reign here in this situation!"

Praying in this way is remarkably free of striving. We are not seeking to impose our own will but to facilitate His reign and order. We can pray in this way if we are sure of our rights as ambassadors; remember, He appointed you to the position, so you are qualified!

See the difference in the following scenarios.

- "Lord, if it be Your will, please heal Maria's arm."

- "Lord, it is Your will to heal, and You have given us Your authority to decree right order here. Arm, be healed in Jesus's name; come into divine order."

It seems to me that one of those praying above is unsure of their position, and the other is praying with confidence.

I really want to encourage you to pray in the Spirit, in tongues. It's true that there are times when we don't know what to pray or how to pray, but as we pray in tongues the Holy Spirit decrees through us His solutions, His way into the situation.

Do you want to hear a funny story? It's true. One time I was praying for a guy who asked for prayer because—now this is a little embarrassing—he had a problem with flatulence. The smells just kept coming, bless him! As I and another prayed for him, the Lord gave us a word. It's deep, it's theological. Ready?

"Baked beans."

There you have it. The Holy Spirit knew that he was simply eating too many baked beans in tomato sauce, resulting in turbo power on the flatulence meter! No fuss, just a solution.

If you do not as yet pray in tongues, ask the Holy Spirit for the gift and begin to open your mouth, uttering the sounds that come. Your mind will scream at you that you are being foolish and that you are a fake. Satan knows full well the price he is going to pay for your newly discovered armory.

The Holy Spirit wants to pray with and through you.

Do you want to ask Him for that gift now? Let's pray if you do.

First, affirm with Him that you are completely His, that you have renounced sin and that you want Him to have free reign in your life. Then you might pray:

> *Lord Jesus, thank You for Your love and for Your empowering gifts. I want to pray effectively, Lord, but at times I don't know what or how to pray.*

Please give me the gift of speaking in tongues. Thank You!

Just begin to open your mouth and utter sounds that seem natural to you. Push through. Get over your thinking, and you will see how, step by step, He develops this gift in you.

To coin a phrase from the popular game show *Who Wants to Be a Millionaire?*, the Cross is the "final answer." Jesus has won the victory over sin and darkness, and we can use His name, having identified with His death and resurrection, to establish His order where light is needed. Prayer can be an adventure!

14

A TRIP TO THE MOVIES—
THE TRUMAN SHOW
(TRUE-MAN IDENTITY)

T*HE TRUMAN SHOW* is a 1998 American satirical, comedy drama film directed by Peter Weir and written by Andrew Niccol. The cast includes Jim Carrey as Truman Burbank, and the film chronicles the life of a man who is initially unaware that he is living in a constructed reality television show broadcast around the clock to billions of people across the globe. Truman becomes suspicious of his perceived reality and embarks on a quest to discover the truth about his life.

The film was a financial and critical success and has been analyzed as a thesis on Christianity, simulated reality, and the rise of reality TV.

WE ALL WANT REALITY

Truman's life is filmed through thousands of hidden cameras, twenty-four hours a day, seven days a week, and broadcast live around the world, allowing the executive producer (Christof) to capture Truman's real emotion and human behavior when put in certain situations. Truman's hometown of Seahaven is a complete film set built under a giant arcological dome, populated by the show's actors and crew, allowing Christof to control every aspect of Truman's life, even the weather. To prevent Truman from discovering his false reality, Christof has invented means of dissuading his sense of exploration, including "killing" his father in a storm while on a fishing trip as a young boy to instill in him a fear of water, making many news reports and "commercials" about the dangers of traveling, and also featuring television shows about how good it is to stay at home.

However, despite Christof's control, Truman behaves in unexpected ways, in particular, falling in love with an actress, an "extra'" known to Truman as Lauren. Meryl, the character intended to be his wife, gamely attempts to make their relationship work, but Truman's heart is clearly elsewhere. Though Lauren is removed from the set quickly, her memory still resonates with him, and he "secretly" thinks of her outside of his marriage to Meryl. Lauren shortly afterward becomes part of a "Free Truman" campaign that fights to have Truman freed from the show.

Truman is in bondage. His almost perfect life is a sham. He has not "met" reality. I wonder how many of us have had, or have, facets of our lives that have fit—or that fit—such a description?

Back to the show. During the thirtieth year of *The Truman Show* Truman begins to notice certain aspects of his near-perfect world that seem out of place, such as a falling spotlight, from the artificial night sky con- stellations, that nearly hits him (quickly passed off by local radio as an aircraft's dislodged landing light) and Truman's car radio accidentally picking up conversation between employees of the show's crew. As well as these strange one-off occurrences, Truman also becomes aware of more subtle abnormalities within his regular day-to-day life, such as the way in which the same people appear in the same places at certain times each day and Meryl's tendency to blatantly advertise the various products she buys. These eye-opening events include the shocking reappearance of Truman's supposedly "dead" father on the film set, at first dressed as a tramp. The old man is suddenly whisked away as soon as Truman notices him. In a deleted scene Truman gives a sandwich to a wheelchair-bound man and then sees him jogging two days later. When the man denies everything, Truman points out he was wearing the same running shoes with the taped initials attached.

All these events cause Truman to start wondering.

It's healthy when we take time out to consider the amazing gospel that we have become part of and to do a reality check. Lord, I want to experience the fullness of Your Life. This Life cost You everything. Your blood flowed that I might know Your glory.

Truman wonders about his life, realizing how the world seems to revolve around him. He seeks to get away from Seahaven but is blocked time and time again.

We have an enemy who would seek to keep us in the dark, to keep us unaware of who we have become in Jesus Christ and unaware of the potential of our destinies.

Truman is frustrated by his inability to arrange for flights, bus breakdowns, sudden masses of traffic, a forest fire, and even (so desperate is Christof to keep him from discovering the truth) an apparent nuclear meltdown, which Truman believes until the policeman, whom Truman had never met before, *calls him by name.*

Piece by piece Truman's false world is beginning to

dismantle. You know, the Holy Spirit is going to dismantle all that is fake about our lives too. He wants us free!

> Now the Lord is the Spirit, and where the Spirit of the Lord is, there is liberty.
>
> —2 CORINTHIANS 3:17

One night Truman manages to fool the cameras and escapes the basement undetected via a secret tunnel, forcing Christof to temporarily suspend broadcasting of the show for the first time in its history. This causes a surge in viewership, with many viewers cheering on Truman's escape attempt!

I trust that you have a good insight into the tone of this movie, courtesy of Wikipedia![1]

I trust that you can see why I am spending some time focusing on this particular film.

I really was captivated by it, and it remains one of my favorites to this day. It's constructed upon a remarkable premise and is packed with imagery and symbolism. I would strongly encourage you to see it (buy it for a discount price at one of those famous online retailers!) and allow the Holy Spirit to talk to you about two major themes in our lives: *identity* and *reality*.

May we go back a step?

I have no hesitation in saying that I consider the teaching of the theory of evolution as a "fact" to be responsible for a swathe of identity issues in society, including our kingdom of God society. This notion that somehow each of us emerged into some kind of random, purposeless existence (except to exist and multiply) underlies much of the value systems that not only surround us but also that lie deep in our psyches.

You see, we are all born looking for home. Each person born on our planet arrives with an innate need to belong; the truth is that we do belong to our Creator, although at some point in our lives we will each need to affirm our paid-for redemption back to Him through Christ Jesus. Until we each do so, we remain in and under the domain of darkness, outside Christ and outside that identity that God has for us.

Once redeemed through the blood of Jesus we have access to our Father. We, like the prodigal son, *have come home*, and God wants us to—and calls us to—enjoy all that He is and all that He has under His roof.

Some of us tend to live from an orphan spirit; we have arrived home, have been adopted into the family of God, but somehow the reality of it has not taken root in us. We flounder with direction, have a sense of rootlessness; we are not really sure who we are or what we are born to do, and we cover the pain with activity and busyness.

We were individually fashioned in our mother's womb, *whatever the circumstance of that conception*. Only in God's mind could apparently dubious circumstances, which may surround your background, intertwine beautifully to form a unique mosaic that is entitled, were it to be displayed in a gallery, *You*. In Jesus, all things are made new.

> For You formed my inward parts;
> You wove me in my mother's womb.
> I will give thanks to You, for I am fearfully and
>   wonderfully made;
> Wonderful are Your works,
> And my soul knows it very well.
> My frame was not hidden from You,
> When I was made in secret,
> And skillfully wrought in the depths of the earth;

Your eyes have seen my unformed substance;
And in Your book were all written
The days that were ordained for me,
When as yet there was not one of them.

—PSALM 139:13–16

Here it is in The Message:

Oh yes, you shaped me first inside, then out;
  you formed me in my mother's womb.
I thank you, High God—you're breathtaking!
  Body and soul, I am marvelously made!
  I worship in adoration—what a creation!
You know me inside and out,
  you know every bone in my body;
You know exactly how I was made, bit by bit,
  how I was sculpted from nothing into
    something.
Like an open book, you watched me grow from
    conception to birth;
  all the stages of my life were spread out before
    you,
The days of my life all prepared
  before I'd even lived one day.

Truman does not know who he is, and there is no freedom for him in his ignorance.

DAWNING OF REVELATION

The glory of the movie, for me, is how, little by little, Truman begins to become aware that this "reality" around him is suspect. It dawns on him, slowly. Peter Weir—I tip my hat to you, sir; the development of this awareness within Truman is beautifully depicted and orchestrated.

Cracks start to appear in the unreality that has been his

world and his life. And his sense of dissatisfaction and suffocation that have largely remained under the surface of his experience surface.

Life is like that, isn't it? Life is full, it is busy, and it offers experience, stimulation, activity, and noise. These things can keep us "deaf" to who we really are for a long time. I thank God for the wonderful Holy Spirit; He finds ways to get in touch with the real us, deep inside, and how to get through to each of us. He is truly magnificent and awesome.

This chapter has already unveiled much of what makes up *The Truman Show*, but have no fear; I am *not* going to reveal the outcome of Truman's search for his true identity!

God wants us to know the power of the Cross in each of our lives. He wants us to know who we really are. He does not want us to live a shadow of the life He bought for us through Jesus. In Him we have become sons. We have not been born into a religion. If that is what we are living, He has *so much* more for us. The Holy Spirit is ready and willing to reveal to you and me the riches of our inheritance in Christ—this is for *now*. Of course, it will be for eternity. But our eternal Life *has already begun*. When we leave this world, we will simply transfer location, and the Life of Christ in us will just go right on living!

As with Truman's unwrapping of the fake world surrounding him, secure as it may have been in one sense, God wants to do the same for us, He wants to unwrap what is not kingdom in our lives, unwrap and dismantle fake securities, dissolve from us molds that have been put there by ourselves and others, reveal to our core who we really are and what has really happened through our association with the Cross and through our birth as a child of God. It is a sensational, stupendous deliverance from "existing" into Life—the glorious Life of Christ.

15

THE SCENT OF THE GOSPEL

SMELLS. AROMAS AND scents. I love them. Some of my favorites will be some of yours. Some of mine might be yours. And with some we might be polarized in our difference of opinion and taste!

Here is a list of some of my favorite smells and scents, in a somewhat random order, I confess; I wonder how many of them you enjoy.

- Newly laid tar on the road
- Freshly brewed coffee
- Petrol (gasoline) (yep!)
- Freshly baked bread
- Inside and around a football stadium
- Freshly roasted meat
- A vast range of eau de toilettes and aftershaves
- Strawberries
- Freshly cut grass
- Leather

- A new car!

- A dog after a bath

On the other hand, smells that I really do *not* like include:

- Hot rice pudding

- Hot milk

- Body odor (sorry, but it's true) and halitosis (bad breath)

- Indian curry

- Gooseberries

- Primary schools (anyone know what I mean?)

- Hospitals

- Glue

- A dog that really needs a bath!

Mmm, the more I consider the latter list, I have to admit there are some odd ones in there, and no offense is intended to anyone who works in or has to stay in hospitals!

Smells are very evocative, don't you think? They are powerful; a brief waft of a certain scent can "take you" somewhere; a memory is recalled, emotions roused, and moments are briefly but potently recalled and perhaps relived.

This morning (as I write) I walked past the swimming pool at my place of work, and a breath of chlorine came my way; instantly I recalled my fears as a youngster of efforts made to teach me to swim. I was afraid of water. Very afraid! A single scent is all that is required to remind me of that sense of insecurity that I experienced so strongly.

The smell of a sizzling hamburger at a street vendor makes me smile. Apart from my enjoyment of such "healthy" delight, I recall the smells that accompanied by first visits to West Ham United Football Club. Street sellers lined, and still line, the route to the stadium, feeding the faithful, evoking a collective feast. Those scents are wrapped up in the thrill of those occasions, and I imagine I will hold them dear forever.

Put it like this; there are smells that edify and enliven us and smells that cause us to balk.

EAU DE GOSPEL

It is the same with the true gospel of Jesus Christ, as Paul writes:

> But thanks be to God, who always leads us in triumph in Christ, and manifests through us the sweet aroma of the knowledge of Him in every place. For we are a fragrance of Christ to God among those who are being saved and among those who are perishing; to the one an aroma from death to death, to the other an aroma from life to life.
>
> —2 CORINTHIANS 2:14–16

Jesus Christ is the chief cornerstone of all that God builds in our lives. The underlying foundation to all that He works in us is set for eternity:

> For no man can lay a foundation other than the one which is laid, which is Jesus Christ.
>
> —1 CORINTHIANS 3:11

Paul says that he preaches Christ and Him crucified. Paul's identity was entwined in Jesus. He had nothing of his own wisdom to boast of; he knew he could add nothing to the finished work of the Cross. And it was as he lived from that place that God worked awesomely through him.

The Holy Spirit

Paul had previously taken great pride in his birth, in his learning, and in his religious elevation. Meeting Jesus, he saw that it was comparatively worthless and Lifeless.

We have Jesus to thank for all that is built in the kingdom. The Holy Spirit is a wonderful Person. He is God. He is no less than God Himself.

The Holy Spirit is the *very scent* of God. In His essence He is God; He is Lord. He is not just a power, He is not just a presence, and He is not just an out-worker of heavenly things and of signs and wonders. *He is the Lord Himself.*

All that He is doing He does because of the Cross. After Jesus was crucified and raised from the dead, between which events Jesus descended into hell and took back the authority lost in Eden, the Holy Spirit was released to fill every man who would receive Him, to fill men and make them new, birthing them into a new identity.

As we live that life, as the earlier scripture testifies, we are, to many, the scent of hope. To others that may not and will not be the case.

But I see that in the church there will be those who embrace the Spirit Life and others who will prefer to live from their own resources. There will also be those in the church, eager to press on in their spiritual walk, who will say, "It's time to move on from the Cross. That was fine as a foundation, but we need to progress into new truths."

But let me say that *everything* that God brings us into, every door He opens for us, and every revelation that becomes ours from heaven stems from the Cross and *has its Life in the Cross.*

Paul says in Hebrews:

> Therefore leaving the elementary teaching about the Christ, let us press on to maturity, not laying again a foundation of repentance from dead works and of faith toward God, of instruction about washings and laying on of hands, and the resurrection of the dead and eternal judgment.
>
> —HEBREWS 6:1–2

He is not telling us to forget about the Cross or to move on from it. To "leave the elementary teachings" means to settle them once for all in our hearts and minds! And then, from there, to *appropriate* all that God has for us, all that He has destined us for!

We need to, and can, live as kingdom people, as sons and daughters of the King who know who they are in Jesus. This Life is built on the unshakable Cross.

There is nothing proud or haughty about knowing who you truly are in Christ. Pride separates us from reality. That's what happened to Lucifer. He allowed pride to get the better of him. He thought he knew better than God and then tried to impose his will over God's will; he attempted to usurp God's order with one of his own.

Those who determine that they are not worthy of Jesus's affection, grace, and redemption are yielding to pride. They are preferring disorder to divine order.

If I adopt you as my son or daughter, declare you to be mine and, as such, *worthy of* and *welcome to* all of my assets, *even to participating in my nature,* and your response is to say, "No, this is not so. I am not worthy to live in this way for such-and-such a reason," then you are—to be frank—rebelling against the right order I have established in adopting you. You are giving yourself an excuse *not* to participate in, enjoy, and grow in all that I have provided for you. The Father heart does not condemn those who so respond, but He grieves that this person is unnecessarily disqualifying himself or herself from an abundant kingdom Life.

I confess, I want it all! I want my entire inheritance in Jesus. I believe the way to loose it into my life is to live simply in His Life. If it were complicated, children may not be able to manage it, but it is they we are told to imitate.

I believe that we are living in days where He is especially accessible. He does not want to withhold Himself from us; indeed, he has already given Himself to us, fully. Days are now approaching when the true church of Jesus is going to be seen. People want to know and see the reality:

> For the anxious longing of the creation waits eagerly
> for the revealing of the sons of God.
>
> —ROMANS 8:19

The Message paraphrases it like this:

> The created world itself can hardly wait for what's coming next.

And the New Century Version says:

> Everything God made is waiting with excitement for God to show his children's glory completely.

It's wonderful to testify to the glory of God, to ascribe Him glory, and to see His glorious acts through the power of the Holy Spirit.

Perhaps we celebrate less often than He takes great joy in glorifying *us*. This is important to grasp as we progress in these latter days. He is coming for a glorious bride, a glorious church. That is you and me. He is coming for a church that lives supernaturally in His glory.

16

END-TIME CHURCH AND THE CROSS

T HIS IS NOT the setting for a detailed explanation of why I, and countless others, believe that we are living in hugely significant days, days often referred to as the Last Days, days that are ushering in or are already part of the end days of this, current earthly reality before the Second Coming of Jesus Christ, the King of kings and undisputed Lord of lords.

I like that word—*undisputed*. It reminds me of a scene in *A Few Good Men* (1992) when the prosecution introduces their case to the court. Certain details are shared and declared to be "undisputed"—they happened and that's final.

We are not waiting for the kingdom of God, in one sense. It is already here, alive and well, being expressed through the lives of millions who have found, and who are finding, new Life and relationship with God in Jesus Christ.

And yet we are looking forward to the unveiling of the glorious kingdom that will take place with the return of Christ to reign and rule, the old order of things being rolled up as "done" and new heavens and a new earth appearing, to remain for all eternity.

If you haven't done so recently, why not take a moment

now to ponder the fact that as one of Christ's own, ransomed and redeemed by His blood, you are going to spend the rest of eternity with Him! I say "the rest of eternity" as eternity has, of course, already begun for us who are in Jesus Christ. This is not something that will happen when we die our natural death. It began when we died with Christ and were raised with Him!

It's amazing how much time we spend planning a vacation, right? We think about it, we drool over the prospect of time away from work in a sun-bleached setting, perhaps by the sea or a pool. We buy the brochures and check out the soon to be enjoyed scenery online. All for a two-week vacation!

Well, how about some alternative dreaming? Heaven is going to be our permanent home! After considerable research I have discovered that eternity is a good deal longer than a fortnight!

You might even want to check out the final destination a little. The Book of Revelation says that all who read it are blessed, so let's be blessed for a moment! Have a look at this brochure!

> And he carried me away in the Spirit to a great and high mountain, and showed me the holy city, Jerusalem, coming down out of heaven from God, having the glory of God. Her brilliance was like a very costly stone, as a stone of crystal-clear jasper. It had a great and high wall, with twelve gates, and at the gates twelve angels; and names were written on them, which are the names of the twelve tribes of the sons of Israel. There were three gates on the east and three gates on the north and three gates on the south and three gates on the west. And the wall of the city

had twelve foundation stones, and on them were the twelve names of the twelve apostles of the Lamb.

The one who spoke with me had a gold measuring rod to measure the city, and its gates and its wall. The city is laid out as a square, and its length is as great as the width; and he measured the city with the rod, fifteen hundred miles; its length and width and height are equal. And he measured its wall, seventy-two yards, according to human measurements, which are also angelic measurements. The material of the wall was jasper; and the city was pure gold, like clear glass. The foundation stones of the city wall were adorned with every kind of precious stone. The first foundation stone was jasper; the second, sapphire; the third, chalcedony; the fourth, emerald; the fifth, sardonyx; the sixth, sardius; the seventh, chrysolite; the eighth, beryl; the ninth, topaz; the tenth, chrysoprase; the eleventh, jacinth; the twelfth, amethyst. And the twelve gates were twelve pearls; each one of the gates was a single pearl. And the street of the city was pure gold, like transparent glass.

I saw no temple in it, for the Lord God the Almighty and the Lamb are its temple. And the city has no need of the sun or of the moon to shine on it, for the glory of God has illumined it, and its lamp is the Lamb. The nations will walk by its light, and the kings of the earth will bring their glory into it. In the daytime (for there will be no night there) its gates will never be closed; and they will bring the glory and the honor of the nations into it; and nothing unclean, and no one who practices abomination and lying, shall ever come into it, but only those whose names are written in the Lamb's book of life.

—REVELATION 21:10–27

I think we could call that five-star-plus accommodation.

Of course, those separated from Him will also continue in that state once their earthly days are complete.

We will all change location in the sense that we will no longer be confined to our current physical forms. In the kingdom of God we will continue to live in Him and with Him, and, finally, we will be liberated from our existing bodies and clothed in new ones that bear us no ills or limitations.

The Bible describes these last days as treacherous, but where sin abounds, grace will abound to that degree and more:

> The Law came in so that the transgression would increase; but where sin increased, grace abounded all the more.
>
> —ROMANS 5:20

It is a kingdom principle that where darkness operates, God can outshine it. His hands are never tied, and He is never limited.

When we look at what is happening around us in the twenty-first century, we have ample evidence that human nature is incapable of improvement. History shows us, in many ways and through events in many nations, that fallen human nature is hopelessly lost and utterly decayed. That is not to say that, made in the image of God, men do not try and, indeed, labor earnestly to bring remedies to our sick world, sick politics, sick business, sick economies, and fragile relationships.

We are going to witness an ever-deepening desperation among the nations of the world. In many respects, the cry for solutions rivals the cries for pleasure and escape, as humanity stumbles its way along its Christ-free path. Meanwhile, the Holy Spirit is powerfully at work, drawing His children into an ever-growing intimacy so that they might be the prophetic voices and hands that demonstrate the power of the kingdom of God.

TRAINING

For some of you reading today, it has been a long walk. You have had many trials. It has been painful. There have been days and even seasons when you felt completely clueless about how you were going to keep going in your walk of faith, such were the circumstances arrayed against you. Perhaps you could identify with the Jonah:

> Water encompassed me to the point of death. The great deep engulfed me, weeds were wrapped around my head.
>
> —JONAH 2:5

But here you are. You are alive. Jesus is alive in you. You have not surrendered. You have not been overcome. Despite it *all* you know whose you are and that the Holy Spirit resides in you and that the last part of your story has not been told.

I believe that the Father wants to put His arms around you even now. He wants to hold your head gently and look you intently in the eyes. He wants to assure you of His love and of His deep delight in you. "Well done, good and faithful one. You don't think you have been faithful, not faithful enough, but I am not measuring you as you do. I know the measure of Me in you, and we are winning. Keep your eyes on Me, even now. *We win!*"

For some of you the hardest part has been those unanswered questions: "Why, Lord?"

Our need to know is understandable, but actually this is part of our old nature. The truth is that we don't really need to know. When we ask Him why, He will often not answer us but pose us a question in return: "What now? What are you going to do now? Are you going to choose endless reasoning and frustration, or My peace that comes through simply deciding to trust?

Everything that God works in us is built to last. He is committed to dismantling all that He has not planted and all that binds us from experiencing the freedom He set us free to enjoy. He doesn't do it all at once; He does it differently in each of us, unique as we are.

He works in us to conform us to the image of Jesus. I think we misunderstand this sometimes. He is not trying to bring a controlling conformity among us, His people. He wants us to be radically and gloriously unique! We glorify Him by getting freed up to be able to express the person He has created us to be; thus, together, this freedom builds the kingdom and a magnificent expression of the Creator God through His church, the bride truly reflecting the glory of the Husband as she yields to His love and invests herself in Him. He has completely invested Himself in us.

You cannot be truly you in Christ Jesus and conflict with Christ's nature. I am preaching to myself, and I like that!

The Cross demonstrates His investment in us. Even while we were separated from Him, without an inkling of the kingdom, without the merest desire of giving the Creator place in our lives, He deigns to pay the ultimate price and buy us back. We are truly that treasure in the field that the Master sold all He had to purchase, knowing that we, buried there, were worth it, worth retrieving and worth restoring. (See Matthew 13.)

GLORY IN THE CHURCH

Our selfless Lord and friend, Jesus Christ, said some amazing things about us before He went to the Cross. We have already seen these verses, but I want to focus on glory as well as unity.

> The glory which You have given Me *I have given to them, that they may be one, just as We are one;* I in them and You in Me, that they may be perfected in unity, *so that the world may know* that You sent Me, and loved them, even as You have loved Me.
> —JOHN 17:22–23, EMPHASIS ADDED

Jesus has glorified us with the same glory with which the Father endowed the Son. This is a staggering truth! A born-again believer, filled with the Holy Spirit, is a walking, talking "God presence." This is what a prophetic, proclamatory church can look like. We walk in the Holy Spirit and live each day from the heavenly places where we have been placed, allowing revelation to come to us, that we may express Him in our thoughts, words, and deeds. We live in His authority, declaring divine order to the disorders that come across our paths. This is a long way from following a religion.

This is the Life of Christ living through us. We can expect to know things that no person has told us, because He told us. We can expect Him to bring about divine appointments where we have a window of opportunity, maybe even just a few minutes, to encourage someone, to advise them, to make them laugh, to pray for them, to restrain them, to hold them.

Praying for someone doesn't have to be a "big deal." Do it like *you* do it. Be you. I like to look at someone in the eye, simply bring Jesus into their situation, and let His love do His work. There probably will not be too many situations where you are going to kneel, lift your hands in the air, and screw your eyes tightly shut before launching out in tongues!

You may pray for someone in secret (it is usually this way, I expect) and then hear of their healing, restoration, or deliverance. You may pray for someone with your church (as we have often done and often do) and rejoice in answers to prayer: cancer healed, relationships mended, a lost item found, a visa accepted and processed, an exam passed, a job obtained, an emotional breakthrough confirmed. Lives are touched in a myriad of ways.

It's not a floorshow. We have nothing to prove, for ourselves. We already have His approval, so I guess that frees up you and me to just go and love some people. It's His love that carries life-changing power.

I love it when I preach and people get revelation! It must be Him! I love it when I pray for someone and they get healed! It must be Him! I love playing soaking music or just playing my keyboard in the Holy Spirit, and we get revelation from Him. He moves in the music and then shares it with us. Oh my, You are so good, Lord!

The Cross has reconciled us to God, to the Father through Jesus. As ambassadors we take that identity, that citizenship, one that has been bestowed with the very glory of Jesus, to every place where our feet tread.

Ambassadors have significant authority. Can I encourage you to dream big dreams? You and I may never be famous, but our fame is already recognized in heaven, where we are known as His sons and daughters.

This glory that has been placed within us may express itself, at times, in ways that dumbfound us. Let's not resist Him.

I want to see more of His glory and more of the glory that He says He has given me. I know the anointing. I know prophetic revelation from the Spirit, but I would like to grow more, especially in areas such as healing the sick and discernment.

This glory will hide you when need be. It will thrust you into the limelight if it serves kingdom purposes.

The supernatural realm in which we live, in which we have been placed, is going to become more real to us, more evident in our daily activities and exchanges with people. Expect to become more aware of angelic activity and support as you go about your day. Would you like a testimony about an angel?

A friend of mine was driving along a dual highway (two lanes) at night. She was going to pull right to overtake a car in front of her when she heard a voice *from the back of her car.*

"Don't!"

At that moment a car sped past her on the wrong side of the central median with no lights on. She probably would have died. Lord, You really are closer to us than we can imagine!

An ordinary day will never be ordinary in the way that the world may describe it. We are supernatural, glorified, walking in the Holy Spirit whether we are cleaning the floor, driving the car, taking a shower, leading a meeting, having coffee, playing with the kids, making love, preaching, or *whatever*! Let's go with the flow of the Holy

Spirit. Let's move with Him. Let's invite the kingdom in all that we are and in all that we do! Ask the Lord to open your spiritual eyes and ears to His realm. You and I are agents of the kingdom of God.

Invite Him into your dream life—expect Him to speak into your dreams and to give you revelation about your life and about the sphere of influence you move in.

I have had many "God" dreams! Many many many! I am so grateful for them. I met a couple of angels in one dream. Let me tell you.

I had been concerned about various turns of events in an area of my life. I don't need to go into the details. Suffice it to say that I had been bringing these things to the Lord and asking Him to fully exercise His Lordship in them and to bring me through.

In the dream I left a building and stepped outside. I stepped into a puddle and heard myself say something like, "Oh typical!" I guess it was an expression of my inner angst. At that moment I stopped and my head looked up. I closed my eyes and I was lifted from my feet. I am aware that an encounter is taking place!

Then I find myself sitting in a chair, my eyes still closed. My hands are on the armrests of the chair. A hand is placed on each of my hands. I can feel them so I know that there are two angels with me. The angel to my left speaks: "Ah, things haven't worked out as you expected."

Next, the angel tells the other angel that it is time for them to go. As they leave and as I start to wake up, I can *still physically feel the touch of one of the hands on my hand.* Despite the fact that little was said, I awoke knowing that *He knew, the kingdom knew* where I was, and that was enough for me.

Lord, You are wonderful, and we cannot box You in at all. Why would we want to?

God will lead you, guide you, and express Himself in you and through you. He will open and shut doors. Sometimes you may welcome His interaction, and at other times it may be inconvenient. He has done this for me many times. His favor does that for us. His favor plants us and keeps us. He shields us and can make us invisible and very visible! It's an adventure! He is meticulous in His detailed supervision and oversight of you and your life. He may delay you or advance you.

You see, He knows!

And it is all thanks to the Cross.

Can we pray?

> *Lord Jesus, thank You for making me Your son through the Cross and for raising me to heavenly places with You. You have seated me in a place of authority. You have called me to exercise authority as a son and as an ambassador. You have called me to decree kingdom order and to decree a stop to disorder within my sphere of influence.*
>
> *You have given me the glory that You have. I will not say I am unworthy of it, for You have made me completely worthy through the blood of the Cross. You have shared Your glory with me, so I welcome the expression of Your glory in my life.*
>
> *Lord, help me please to grow in my identity and to live in step with the Holy Spirit. Thank You for the foundation of the Cross in my life, one that is at the root of all You are doing in me.*

*Lord, I welcome Your revelation so that I may
walk in Life, in truth, and in intimacy with You.
Thank You, Lord Jesus. Amen.*

We will *never* outgrow the Cross.

In Him we have redemption through His blood,
the forgiveness of our trespasses, according to the
riches of His grace which He lavished on us. In
all wisdom and insight He made known to us the
mystery of His will, according to His kind intention which He purposed in Him with a view to an
administration suitable to the fullness of the times,
that is, *the summing up of all things in Christ, things
in the heavens and things on the earth.* In Him also
we have obtained an inheritance.
—Ephesians 1:7–11, emphasis added

Because of the sacrifice of the Messiah, his blood
poured out on the altar of the Cross, we're a free
people—free of penalties and punishments chalked
up by all our misdeeds. And not just barely free,
either. Abundantly free! He thought of everything,
provided for everything we could possibly need,
letting us in on the plans he took such delight in
making. He set it all out before us in Christ, a long-
range plan in which everything would be brought
together and summed up in him, everything in
deepest heaven, everything on planet earth.
—Ephesians 1:7–10, The Message

The Cross is still the crux of the matter.

Postscript

PASSION

Hows your passion?
What are your passions in life? Who is your passion?

What does that feel like? How have your passions impacted the decisions you have been making?

I would just like to leave you with an invitation to bring your passions to Jesus.

He has created us to live passionate lives. We have seen that the Passion of Christ stemmed from His passion for His Father and for us.

We—you—are so deeply loved. God is for you. He is on your side. He is your greatest fan. His passion for you is stirred when He sees you, thinks about you, and relates to you.

He does not talk to you because He is obliged to do so by some self-imposed religious duty. He wants to put His hands all over you and hold you.

Men? He wants to look you in the eye and say, "You are already good enough, already more than accepted. You fit the bill, son. Let's have some adventure!"

Ladies? He wants to look you in the eye too. "You are beautiful. You are mine. You are unique and equipped to make waves in this world with Me. Let's go and rescue some people!"

If you feel that your experience of His passion for you has faded, or that your own passion for Him is less than you would like to experience, please simply bring that to Him. Please do not miss the point and switch into striving mode: "I had better pray more, go to more meetings, try harder, read 'x' number of Bible chapters each day."

Praying, meeting with Him among other believers, and musing on His Word are excellent things to do. But let them issue from love. He loves you. If you never pick up your Bible again, you will miss some of His messages and gifts, but He will not love you any less.

I remember something from my relatively early days as a Christian. I was part of a lively, charismatic Christian fellowship, where there was much to enjoy and to be part of in the Holy Spirit. I am grateful for that hive of the Spirit to this day.

But I lacked self-assurance in those days and fell into striving mode from time to time. On one occasion a friend said this to me. It's probably almost word for word as he spoke it: "Steve, I think the real Steve is a terrific guy. I think the Steve with the mask on is pathetic."

I think you can reliably call that a Holy Spirit "ouch!" But it was true. And because it was said with the motive and intention of bringing me into freedom in Jesus, it served a useful purpose.

Jesus loves you passionately. He wants you to experience this in your life. As you receive and experience His love, the love that has already been shed abroad in your heart by the Holy Spirit will burn for Him and for others (Rom. 5:5).

He bled for you, rose for you, and has glorified you.

There is much to expect in the days to come!

BLESSING

Now to Him who is able to keep you from stumbling, and to make you stand in the presence of His glory blameless with great joy, to the only God our Savior, through Jesus Christ our Lord, be glory, majesty, dominion and authority, before all time and now and forever. Amen.

—JUDE 24–25

Appendix

HAVE YOU MET HIM YET?

As I write, the specification description on TV sets of "HD Ready" is already superseded, on many models, by "Full HD." HD means 'High Definition' for the as yet uninitiated.

My own TV is HD Ready. Were I to upgrade my "not so technical" brain and find the inclination to equally upgrade my equipment, I would be able to benefit from a sharper, clearer picture.

God offers you a revolutionary upgrade to your life, whether you are satisfied with your current model or not. May I ask you a question?

Are you Heaven Destination ready?

You and I can be. We can live from a place where we are ready, in a moment, in the twinkling of an eye, to move from our present, temporary stay here on earth to a permanent kingdom destination.

If we already have a relationship with Jesus, regardless of its potency, the fact is that we are already seated in heavenly places. Our earthly "death," whenever that may occur, will merely see us transferred from one domain to another. Our physical body, having ceased to function, will mean that we can no longer live on this earth, and our spirit man will continue to live in heaven. And it will be clothed in a new heavenly body, which will not be overweight, aching, painful, nonfunctioning, or tired!

Nevertheless, the Lord would have us live right now from those heavenly places; this will maximize our wondrous experience of Him on earth and also, as a springtime fragrance, spread kingdom influence here around us.

For those reading who have never invited Jesus to "take them on" in this life and who, like the famous woman at the well (John 4), may perhaps be tired of trying to make it in this life under their own steam, please consider this opportunity to take part in an exchange. You are offered a *divine* exchange.

Divine Exchange

Become heaven ready. Cross over the bridge from a life without Christ to the kingdom of God. Don't be tempted to "go all holy," to pray something clever or to change your clothes or hairstyle. If you recognize that you are not living His Life and would like to, here is a chance for you.

You and I were born separated from God. Jesus bridged that separation by taking the penalty for your and my condition (and our subsequent actions) on the Cross. He paid that debt. He paid your debt whether you recognize it or not, but you need to redeem your coupon to partner in what He did. It would be a sad waste if the coupon with your name on it remained unused, or unredeemed.

If this resonates with you, I would like to invite you to simply and genuinely pray with me the following prayer. It may seem a small step for you, but believe me, the step that God is taking toward you is enormous and, you are going to wonderfully discover, life-changing Life.

> *Lord Jesus, I believe that You died on the Cross and shed Your blood to settle the penalty of my separation from You. Please forgive me for all that I have done wrong, deliberately or otherwise. Likewise I am ready to forgive any and all who have hurt me. As You freely forgive me, I equally release others.*
>
> *I gratefully receive Your forgiveness. Please come into my life as my Lord and Savior. Holy Spirit, come into my life and "take me on."*
>
> *You promised to make me new. Yes, Lord, come in and do that; reveal more and more of Yourself to me through the Bible, through other Christians, and through Your Holy Spirit.*
>
> *Thank You, Lord Jesus. Amen.*

Congratulations if you have prayed this and meant it! God has kept His side and done something supernatural in your life.

If you found it difficult to sincerely forgive someone, just bring that to Him. As you are willing, He will work in your life and help you to release those who have meant you harm. He knows everything about you (Ps. 139) and knows how to get through to you. We need to understand that forgiveness matters. Proverbs 18:19 says:

> A brother offended is harder to be won than a strong city, and contentions are like the bars of a citadel.

We suffer when we do not forgive. We might think that we are holding power over the one who has offended us, but the reality is that the offense is holding us captive. Proverbs 19:8 states:

> He who gets wisdom loves his own soul; he who
> keeps understanding will find good.

Verse 11 reads:

> A man's discretion makes him slow to anger, and it
> is his glory to overlook a transgression.

You and I are on a journey of discovering His miracle-working power in many aspects of life. But the greatest miracle is that He, upon our confession and acceptance of Him, has transferred us from one kingdom to His kingdom. You are Heaven Destination ready. How wonderful!

Just as hot coals need other hot coals around them to maintain their temperature, I would encourage you to seek out a friendly, Bible-believing church where the Holy Spirit is welcome to express Himself. God will help you to find a place where you can feel at home and grow in your faith. God's Spirit within you is able to work in your life and bring transformation. You will not be able to do this in your own strength, nor are you designed to attempt to do so.

As a result of your decision to align your life with the Cross and to receive Jesus, many will now rejoice with you, and a few may not.

As I said in a previous chapter, I have a "thing" about scents. Smells. A barbecue, petrol, a newly surfaced road, scents in a forest or garden, fresh coffee. And I confess to taking delight in different perfumes (or shall we say *eau de toilette*) from a gent's point of view. I have quite a few. Scents are evocative, rich, invigorating, and powerful. They change the immediate atmosphere around you. And that's exactly what Holy Spirit wants to do where you are.

May I wish you every blessing in your walk with Jesus Christ—your friend, Lord and Savior, the King of kings and Lord of lords!

NOTES

INTRODUCTION
THE CROSS IS STILL THE CRUX

1. As quoted in "Defining Postmodernism," The Electronic Labyrinth, http://www2.iath.virginia.edu/elab/hfl0242.html (accessed December 6, 2013).

2. *American Heritage Dictionary of the English Language*, fourth edition (N.p.: Houghton Mifflin Company, 2000), s.v. "crux," as viewed at TheFreeDictionary.com, http://www.thefree-dictionary.com/crux (accessed December 6, 2013).

CHAPTER 4
LET'S GET TOGETHER

1. M. Abdulsalam, "The Tolerance of the Prophet Towards Other Religions (Part 1 of 2): To Each to Their Own Religion," IslamReligion.com, February 27, 2006, http://www.islamreligion.com/articles/207/viewall/ (accessed December 6, 2013).

CHAPTER 6
THE CROSS MEANS "WELCOME"

1. "About Schizophrenia," http://www.schizophrenia24x7.com/about-schizophrenia (accessed December 6, 2013).

CHAPTER 7
RESURRECTION AND LIFE

1. SermonNotebook.org, "Mark 10:46–52: Bartimaeus: A Blind Man With 20/20 Vision," http://www.sermonnotebook.org/new%20testament/Mark%2010_46-52.htm (accessed December 6, 2013).

CHAPTER 9
THE POWER OF THE CROSS IN MUSIC

1. "Hark! The Herald Angels Sing" by Charles Wesley. Public domain.

2. "Are You Washed in the Blood?" by Elisha A. Hoffman. Copyright © Words: Public Domain.

Chapter 12
Blood—a Spiritual Issue

1. Roland Buerk, "Blood Problem for Bangladesh Festival," BBC News, January 29, 2004, http://news.bbc.co.uk /2/hi/south_asia/3440799.stm (accessed December 7, 2013).

2. Alex Potter, "Remembrance and Blood: The Ashura Festival in Lebanon," Matador Network, January 9, 2013, http:// matadornetwork.com/abroad/remembrance-and-blood-the-ashura-festival-in-lebanon (accessed December 7, 2013).

3. Answers.com, "Devi Dhura," http://www.answers.com/ topic/devi-dhura (accessed December 7, 2013).

4. Wikipedia.org, s.v. "seal," http://en.wikipedia.org/wiki/ Seal (accessed December 7, 2013).

Chapter 13
Declaring Prayer

1. Wikipedia.org, s.v. "ambassador," https://en.wikipedia. org/wiki/Ambassador (accessed December 7, 2013).

Chapter 14
A Trip to the Movies—The Truman Show (True-Man Identity)

1. Wikipedia.org, s.v. "The Truman Show," http:// en.wikipedia.org/wiki/The_Truman_Show (accessed December 7, 2013).

ABOUT THE AUTHOR

STEVE HAWKINS, AUTHOR of *From Legal to Regal*, teaches English as a Second Language in London, and is part of New Zion Christian Fellowship in Welwyn Garden City. After becoming a Christian, Steve came to realize that aspects of legalism were preventing him from enjoying an abundant experience of Holy Spirit life. He was liberated by the Holy Spirit starting with a visit to Toronto Airport Christian Fellowship. He ministers today by leading worship, preaching, and exercising his prophetic gift. This book follows *From Legal to Regal*.

CONTACT THE AUTHOR

You may contact Steve Hawkins at
steve.hawkins@cheerful.com.